HEADHUNTERS OF THE CORAL SEA

ION IDRIESS

ETT IMPRINT
Exile Bay

This 11th edition published by ETT Imprint, Exile Bay 2024

First published by Angus & Robertson 1940
Reprinted 1941, 1944, 1946, 1947, 1948, 1951, 1955, 1957
First published by ETT Imprint, Exile Bay 2020
Published as an Imprint Classic in 2024

ETT IMPRINT
PO Box R1906
Royal Exchange NSW 1225 Australia

ISBN 978-1-923024-75-5 (pback)
ISBN 978-1-922473-08-0 (ebook)

Cover and internal design by Tom Thompson using original lithographs from shipwreck tales of the *Charles Eaton*.

HOW I CAME TO WRITE THIS BOOK

During wanderings in the Coral Sea I was amazed by the story of two white boys who had lived amongst the islanders many years ago. The story of the capture of the two Lamars, as the white boys were called, and their subsequent adventures until their rescue, had been handed down in legend among the Torres Strait islanders.

It was not until years afterwards that I learned, in civilized society, the other part of the story. The two boys, Jack Ireland and Will D'Oyly, were survivors from the wreck of the *Charles Eaton.* Being already familiar with the native account of the story, it was with the liveliest curiosity that I ferreted out the European account. This is contained in three small pamphlets:

1. *The Melancholy Wreck of the "Charles Eaton"* by Wemyss. This was an account of the wreck so far as was known. The particularly tragic circumstances stirred the Sydney and London of that day.

2. *A Voyage to Torres Strait in Search of the Survivors of the* "Charles Eaton" *wrecked, upon the Barrier Reef in the Month of August 1834, in His Majesty's Colonial Schooner "Isabella"*. C. M. Lewis, Commander. Arranged from the Journal of the Commander by Authority of his Excellency Major-General Sir Richard Bourke, K.C.B., Governor of New South Wales, etc. etc., by Phillip P. King, Captain R.N. This pamphlet contains the account of Captain Lewis who rescued the two boys, but contains a very little of what Jack Ireland told him of his adventures. I wish the good captain had seen fit to include in his narrative much more of the boy's account of his adventures.

3. *Narrative of a Voyage from Sydney to Torres Strait in Search of the Survivors of the "Charles Eaton", in His Majesty's Colonial Schooner "Isabella"* by William Edward Brookett, Sydney. This account is written by a man who sailed aboard the *Isabella.* He, too, includes very little of Ireland's account. But the author and the crew, not understanding the men of Mer or their beliefs and customs, seem to have looked upon young Ireland with pity, but little understanding. He found it difficult to express his thoughts, for he had almost forgotten the English tongue. His rescuers do not seem to have had overmuch patience with the lad.

I now knew the boy's story in its entirety in detail from the story of the islanders; the rescue captain's story, and what little Jack Ireland had told him; the European story of the wreck; and the account of the rescue, by an eye-witness.

Recently my publishers asked me to write "a boy's book".

Immediately I remembered the story of the two boys "rescued from the savages". And here it is. True in every particular, which I hope will add to the value of a book of adventure for boys—from nine to ninety.

The greater part of my material has come from the stories of the Torres Strait islanders themselves, who naturally know by far the greater part of the story. The boys experienced many more adventures than are recorded here, but shortage of paper in these difficult times demands that the story be shortened.

In some respects the remarkable story of these two boys was rather dreadful. I have cut out the most bloodthirsty episodes but must allow some of the grim episodes to remain, otherwise the story would be robbed of truth.

The trading brig *Mangles,* Captain William Carr, commander, which first sighted the boys among the "savages" on Mer Island was owned by a well-known Sydney identity of the time, Captain John Coghill, who then owned a line of trading vessels. One of the old pioneers to take up the Cowpastures, he was a partner of John Boyd, and of Oxley the explorer.

The remarkable belief among the Torres Strait islanders, which saved the life of not only Jack Ireland and Will D'Oyly but of John Sexton and George D'Oyly as well, has been responsible for saving a number of white castaways in the tragic stories of the Strait. Another notable example was Barbara Thompson, saved by the men of Murralug after the wreck of the cutter *America.* Old Piaquai greeted her as the reincarnation of his daughter Giom. She was thus acknowledged by the tribe as one of themselves—a girl come to life again.

The chief Boroto married her as Giom and she lived among the Kowrega tribe for some years until rescued by men of H.M.S. *Rattlesnake.* She, like Jack Ireland, could not recall her language when rescued, beating her forehead in pitiful attempts to answer the questions asked her.

And now to the story of the two boys.

Ion Idriess.

HARLES EATON

The Sailor Boy.
Byron

CONTENTS

CHAPTER	PAGE
THE WRECK	9
THE MASSACRE	15
IN THE HANDS OF THE SKULL-HUNTERS	23
RANSOMED	29
JACK MAKES A FRIEND	34
THE CHALLENGE	38
JACK LEARNS TO FIGHT AND WORK	42
DOWN IN THE UNDERWATER WORLD	48
THE FIGHT AT SEA	54
WHERE THE MUTTON-BIRDS BREED	59
A HAPPY CRUISE	63
THE SHARK	67
THE WHALES	72
DEATH FROM THE DEPTHS	78
THE CYCLONE	82
THE SLEEPERS AT THE GATE	87
THE ATTACK	91
TRAGIC NEWS	94
THE RACE TO SAVE THE FLEET	99
WAR	104
THE LAST STAND	109
A SHIP! A SHIP!	114
RESCUE	121
List of Passengers and Crew	129

ELLMS DEL.

I

THE WRECK

Thunder crashed as the ship trembled, lightning flamed through black skies and dazzled Jack Ireland. He snatched for the mast as the bark rolled sickeningly. To a shuddering thump a wave rolled aboard and Jack clung for life lest he be washed overboard.

As the sky rose and the water swirled away, Jack gasped as he gazed around. Black skies pierced by rain-squalls, lightning flashing upon surging waters, the little bark like a wounded bird tossing on the angry sea. Jack glanced aloft at the wildly swaying masts and noticed that Captain Moore had taken a reef in the topsails. "That means a gale and possible danger," he thought. "It would be terrible if we were shipwrecked in this unknown sea."

And so thought Captain Moore as with the first mate he gazed anxiously from the poop. Old Portland the ship's dog stood beside them.

"I don't like it, Mr Clare," said the captain gravely. "We're feeling our way into nasty weather."

"No, sir", answered the mate.

"And entering the Coral Sea—the most dangerous sea in the world", frowned the captain. "Listen to the seas thundering on the Barrier—like a cannonade in some furious battle. West there through the mists lies the wild Australian coast. Ahead of us lie the thousand reefs and islands of Torres Strait. And those islands peopled by warlike savages."

"At least we are well clear of Mer," replied the mate grimly.

"About one hundred and twenty miles to the south, Mr Clare. But in these uncharted seas with their swift currents we could be swept far out of our course should anything happen."

Both officers stood silent, the safety of the little ship, her passengers and crew heavy upon them. The *Charles Eaton*, a 313-ton bark, bound from Sydney to India, was seeking a passage through the Great Barrier Reef near the extreme north of Queensland. The island of Mer, at which the mate had shuddered, was inhabited by the fiercest and most warlike savages in the Coral Sea. In the Sailing Directions of the day all mariners were warned to give this grim island a wide berth.

Jack Ireland's chum, John Sexton the cabin boy, came staggering across the heaving deck. Against the shriek of the wind he laughed and shouted: "Why look so glum, Jack? We're not food for the fishes yet."

"No, and we won't be," smiled Jack. Then he looked anxious: "I was thinking of Mrs D'Oyly and the two boys", he said.

"That's the worst of it," answered John . . "My word it's difficult to stand against this wind." He tightened his belt.

Mrs D'Oyly, with her quiet smile and gentle ways, was liked by all, while chubby little Will D'Oyly was the ship's favourite. The blue-eyed boy was barely three years old. George D'Oyly was eight, a fine strapping lad, as quiet as his baby brother was lively. Captain D'Oyly, an artillery officer, was returning from leave with his wife and children to his regiment in India.

John Sexton turned towards Jack: "Do you think we're anywhere near Mer?" His shout was almost a whisper.

"Don't know. The bosun said last night that the island lies directly north of here. The captain is now looking for a passage through the great reef here, so that we can steer north again past Sir Charles Hardy Island and carry on along the Australian coast, steering a few points to the west until in Torres Strait we round Cape York ... My word, that was a big one. Look out! Here comes another." They held tight while three big waves rolled by.

"That spray stung my eyes so that I can hardly see," said John. "I thought Captain Moore would be washed from the poop."

"He's having an anxious time," answered Jack. "I'm going below to see if Mrs D'Oyly and the boys need anything."

He waited his chance. To a shrieking gust a mighty wave lifted the ship high, high, higher—they stared into each other's eyes as dizzily she came down —Crash!

With tons of water swirling over them the boys were swept to the ship's side to startled shouts and the frantic bark of Portland. Jack still clung to a rope and snatched at Sexton as they were going overboard. Shudderingly the ship rose up... up... Jack felt the dead weight of water rolling off him; felt his arms being pulled from their sockets as desperately he clung to the rope and to Sexton. Gaspingly he opened his eyes and hung on while the bosun and Jimmy Price dragged them back over the side.

"Run for the poop, lads!" shouted the bosun. "Look out! Hold tight! She's coming!"

To a vision of swaying masts the ship crashed down again, a sickening glimpse of tall masts snapping, coming, coming—to crash across the decks and into the sea. Despairing shouts, splintering decks, scraping of tangled cordage. To the shouts of the captain all hands fought their way to the poop. The ship's keel and rudder were carried away, she fell broadside on, roaring seas sweeping over her. She was a wreck.

"Get ready the boats!" shouted the captain. "Provision them; water them; put aboard arms and ammunition. Then all hands stand by!"

As the dazed sailors sprang to obey orders Jack and John climbed to the poop.

"I'll never forget you, Jack," murmured John.

"It was nothing," mumbled Jack, and hurried to Mrs D'Oyly.

She stood there bravely, her arms around her boys, Captain D'Oyly encouragingly beside her.Mr Armstrong, the young barrister passenger, cracked a joke and she smiled back, clinging to her baby boy. Old Portland gazed sympathetically from big brown eyes. Through the howl of the wind furious seas swirled over the deck below, drenching them with spray. They felt the ship grinding, crunching down on to the reef, until only the poop remained above water. As the men splashed up to the poop Mr Clare whispered to the captain.

"Sorry, sir. All food—water—everything—is now under water." Frantically the men worked at lowering the boats. George Pigott the bosun, with the carpenter Laurie Constantine, and Will Gumble jumped into the dinghy.

"Grab the oars," shouted the bosun. "Fend her off from the ship's side or we'll be smashed. Lower away, boys."

Jimmy Price jumped into the long-boat and snatched an oar just as a shout arose.

"Look out! Look out!"

All hands clung to anything as the ship rolled side-on to a grinding of splintering timbers. There came a despairing shriek as the long-boat was stove in and young Price disappeared beneath the waves. The other boats were crushed, too, except the bosun's boat which broke free and was rapidly being swept away by a current.

"Quick, bosun! To the oars!" shouted the captain, "or you are gone!"

Desperately the three men tried to pull back to the ship, but the current defied their strength. Richard Quin and Joe Wright leaped overboard and swam towards their mates. Both seamen were very powerful swimmers, but soon needed all their strength. The twenty-six half-drowned people on the poop watched with bated breath. Twice the men went under, twice they rose and battled to reach the tossing boat while desperately the men tried to row towards them. At last strong arms seized outstretched hands, and they were hauled aboard. But the boat was being swept farther away.

"No one else attempt that swim," shouted the captain; "it means certain death. We are safer here. If the poop holds together we can build a raft when the weather calms." Cupping his hands he shouted against the wind: "Stand by—if you can. If not—make for Timor."

While they made themselves as secure as possible upon the battered poop, Mr Grant the surgeon did his best to help several men who had been hurt. In misery they watched, as the sun went down, the tiny boat drawing farther and farther away, the bosun and his men struggling to hold her within the shelter of the lee of the reef. Their hearts were in their mouths as they stared at the thunderous seas outside.

"She'll never live!" murmured the captain. "If they are swept from the lee of the reef she'll be swamped."

"Look!" yelled the mate.

And they saw gaunt masts against a blackening sky, a ship with not a sail, yet she seemed to be speeding through foam. As the mists rolled away they sighed in bitter disappointment.

"She's hard and fast upon a reef!" shouted the mate. "She's wrecked too!"

"There doesn't seem to be a soul on board," said the captain. "If only we could reach her!"

As the dinghy rose high upon the wave the bosun also saw the wreck. Desperately his men tried to pull towards her but were held back as if by a giant hand. The dinghy was the plaything of the current and the waves.

"How awful!" shouted Sexton to Jack. "We're wrecked, with the seas breaking over us. And there lies a ship, wrecked too, but high and safe upon a reef. And we cannot reach her!"

Darkness fell. The little crowd huddled together for comfort. A lightning flash showed the dinghy still battling away out there on the waters. Jack Ireland, with his arm comfortingly around young George, felt Mrs D'Oyly shudder. All that night in drenched misery they huddled there listening to the thunder of the waves, feeling the stricken timbers groaning and grinding, expecting them to wrench away beneath their feet—expecting every moment to be their last.

"What will you do?" whispered John in Jack's ear.

"Hang on to George," whispered Jack, "and try and swim with him to a plank when we come up out of the water. Then I'll help Mrs D'Oyly-if I can."

"I'll help you," whispered John.

In a watery dawn the sun shone out in bursts of light drowned by driving mists. The wind had died down but great waves rolled sullenly on the reef.

"Weather is clearing," said the captain hopefully.

"Yes, sir," answered the mate. "We may have a chance."

"If only we could reach that wreck!"

"She's too far to windward," murmured the mate. "Even if we had the long-boat we could not reach her against this wind and current."

They were silent. Far from human aid, in the midst of a wild sea thick with reefs and unknown islands, clinging to the remnant of a wreck from which planks were being torn by wave after wave. Shivering, they stared through the mists.

"She's gone!" said the captain at last. "That is the end of the dinghy. She's either gone under or the currents have swept her away. She has one chance in a hundred. The weather clearing up during the night—they might win out."

They did—after terrible hardships, which killed George Pigott. They reached Timor Laut, in the Dutch East Indies. Were captured and treated as slaves by the Malays. Then rival chiefs fought over them. They were captured again and this time treated kindly. A year later they were rescued by the Dutch. Only then did the fate of the *Charles Eaton* become known. But so slow was communication, so uncertain the adventures of men, that it was more than a year after the wreck that news reached Sydney of what had happened.

On the wrecked ship Jack whispered to John: "I hope they win out—the bosun is aboard."

"So do I," whispered John. "I wish Jimmy Price was with them too."

"Yes. He and the bosun saved our lives."

The castaways were glancing questioningly at Captain Moore.

"In a few days," he said at last, "the seas will have gone down sufficiently to launch a raft. The poop will hold together that long; but it will crumble like a house of cards if a fresh gale blows up. All hands will set to making a raft and provisioning it the best we can. We'll try hard to reach that wreck; but without a boat we may not be able to reach her against these strong currents. In that case, we must take to the sea on the chance of being picked up. If we are not picked up, we must make an island quickly, otherwise we will perish of thirst. Every man get busy." (That abandoned wreck was the *Flora.* If they had reached her, they might have been saved.)

All hands set to with a will, none so hard as the captain and chief mate. Men dived down into the ship and under the mate's instructions managed to bring up a cask, a leaden pipe from the quarter galley cistern, and the ship's coppers. With these the mate fashioned a rough still, and with firewood from the wreck slowly distilled fresh water from the sea. Their only allowance per day was two wine-glasses of distilled water and a few pieces of soppy biscuit. And from this, each put a tiny piece aside for Portland. Then they managed to fish up a cask of pork. In a week the raft was made and launched. With their pitiful supplies all clambered down and—the raft began to sink. It sank until they stood up to their waists in water.

"Better drown in comfort than in misery," said the mate. "Some of us had better lighten the raft, sir; it will give half the party a chance. We can make another."

He clambered back up the wreck and nearly all hands followed him, Jack and John unwillingly.

"Better come with us, lads," said the mate kindly. "It will give the folks on the raft a better chance."

From the battered poop Jack and John and the crew gazed silently down on the raft, wondering if they would ever see any of those people again. Down there, they were up to their knees in water, the captain and Mrs D'Oyly, George and Willie, the Indian woman servant, Captain D'Oyly, George Armstrong, Dr Grant, George Lourne, John Berry and old Portland.

Jack and John gazed down unhappily. George D'Oyly waved up with a smile; Jack and John waved down with a "hurrah!" Mrs D'Oyly smiled back and held up the little boy to wave, sitting there amongst the pitiable belongings on the waterlogged raft.

"Don't cast off, sir," called the mate; "surely we can make the raft more shipshape."

"I'm afraid not, Mr Clare," called up the captain. "We've torn our hands red raw in pulling these few timbers from the wreck. You must make another raft. We'll stand by a while and see if anything can be done. Meanwhile, make your own raft with all speed. If a fresh wind springs up the poop deck will break away. Besides, you *must* put to sea quickly; remember the water question and food. Make north along the Australian coast, veering west for Timor. Whatever you do, don't sail due north or nor'-east from here."

The sun was sinking. The tired men spent themselves trying to wrench out more timber from the wreck, now almost covered by the water. They fell into exhausted sleep at last. In the morning the raft had gone. All hands stared silently. And then—John Sexton pointed. A tiny speck was drifting far away. They stared after her, tears in their eyes.

"John!" whispered Jack, "she's going dead north!" "They can't help it", said John. "The current is carrying the raft away!"

"They're being carried straight towards Mer!" declared a seaman.

All hands were silent.

2

THE MASSACRE

"Come, lads," said the mate briskly, "to breakfast! Then we'll make a raft."

"Bacon and eggs for mine, waiter!" grinned Allan Quail. "Toast just nicely browned, and a dash of cream in the coffee!"

Tommy Cheng crowed like a rooster.

"That's the spirit," laughed the mate. "Now let us dish out this bacon and eggs."

Quietly they swallowed their sloppy biscuit, sipped their mouthful of water. Jack Ireland, John Sexton, and the two midshipmen sat together.

"What do you think of our chances, Jack?" asked Will Perry.

"As good as the chances of any other shipwrecked people."

"We're got to keep our heart up," said John, "and that's all about it."

"It takes a bit of keeping up," said Tommy Cheng, glancing at the forlorn wreck, the rolling sea. "I left old England for adventure," he added, "and I'm certainly getting it."

"We haven't started yet," laughed Jack.

"Come on, lads!" ordered the mate briskly. "All hands set to and we'll build the best raft that ever sailed the seas."

For three days they toiled, wrenching planks from the wreck until they could reach no farther under water, and completed the raft.

"Shall we wait a day or two?" suggested Mr Mayer, the second mate. "It's just possible a British Indiaman may come sailing by."

The men heartily agreed. They waited a week.

"It is hopeless," declared Mr Clare. "We must sail before we perish of thirst."

"We'll perish at the hands of the savages," said a seaman.

"Better a quick death than a lingering one. We launch the raft to-morrow!"

And they did. Mr Clare the chief mate, Mr Mayer the second, Mr Pyall the third, young Jack Ireland and John Sexton cabin boys, little Will Perry and Tommy Cheng the midshipmen, Montgomery the steward, and the seamen: S. Baylett, A. Quad, W. Moore, C. Robinson, J. Caen, W. Hill, W. Jeffrey, J. Miller and W. Williams. Seventeen hands all told. They had hardly drifted away from the wreck than the raft jarred upon the reef cutting lashing and displacing a timber. Then it drifted from the reef with all hands standing knee deep in water, desperately striving to lash the timbers together again.

"We've done the best we can, boys," gasped the mate at last. "Step the mast; rig the sail."

All hands worked with the one desperate thought —"Mer!" They waited with bated breath as the sail slowly filled. Hardly seeming to move, the raft began drifting—nor'-east. They looked at one another.

"A breeze from the Pacific will soon spring up," said Mr Clare cheerily, "and carry us towards the mainland. Then we can sail north, then west towards Timor."

For two days and nights they huddled on the raft, allowed only half a biscuit a man, half a tot of water.

With cramped legs, unspeakably weary, haggard-eyed, they watched a blood-red dawn. There appeared a distant island upon a brazen sea. All stared fearfully. Jack gripped John's arm and pointed. An ominous black fin was cleaving the water behind.

A seaman croaked from thirst-cracked lips. All stared at the shark. It circled the raft with effortless ease and fascinated those on it with cruel, green eyes... Then its fin appeared again, gliding behind.

"Up to our knees in water," croaked a seaman, "and not a gun amongst us. That cunning devil will charge through us any moment. And then—"

"Nonsense!" snapped the mate. "Lash your knives to those poles—quickly now."

Jack looked meaningly at John Sexton. If other sharks should come! All that morning, with their rough lances handy they watched the shark. Ceaselessly he circled the raft, then charged so close that Miller jabbed with his lance.

"Don't thrust unless he charges right in amongst us!" ordered the mate urgently. They crouched back, blanching as the shark charged and Caen lunged forward. The shark disappeared in a swirl of foam.

"My God! you've done it!" cried the mate. A thin trail of blood appeared on the surface.

"Mass in towards the centre," ordered the mate. "Stand back to back. If they come—don't let any break through."

Jack, John, and the midshipmen stood shoulder to shoulder with the men; a hush was upon the sea. A black fin appeared, cruising swiftly. Another and another appeared, tigers of the sea on the scent of blood. Others came. Swiftly they circled the raft, drawing closer and closer, black fins hissing through the water.

Suddenly Robinson shouted. They shivered, with lances ready, but Robinson shouted again, pointing.

A big canoe, with a queer mat sail, and manned with savages, was bearing down upon them, swiftly cleaving the water, the befeathered warriors. glaring at them. A wild yell arose to a waving of clubs. Then silence as the canoe drew alongside.

The shipwrecked mariners stared into the wild eyes of these big, painted savages, their muscular arms banded with shell armlets, and wearing necklets of sharks' teeth. Coronets of long, beautiful feathers bedecked their heads. Some wore queer leggings of split bamboo.

But the boys stood fascinated by the savage chief, towering above his warriors as he glared down upon the raft. Feathers of the sea hawk waved above his tangled hair; his chest was that of a giant. This man was Cut-cut, chief of the Aureed skull-hunters. There have been few more dreaded chiefs in all the history of the Coral Sea. Jack's blood ran cold as malignant eyes glared at him; deep-set eyes made more hideous by broad circles of yellow painted around them. His big mouth snarled in a wide grin. Standing beside Cut-cut was Biskea his lieutenant, his nose flattened from a club blow. Biskea was shorter, but very powerfully built, and with a grin that stretched from ear to ear. Through his flattened nose dangled the foot of a hawk, its talons stretched as if to grip above the thick, cruel lips. He was glaring at John Sexton. Suddenly he shouted "Kabi! Kabi!"

Cut-cut, levelling his club towards Jack, yelled "Wak! Wak!"

The savages glared full upon Jack and John. The crew shivered.

Mr Clare held up his arms, signing peace. He made a motion of drinking. The savages argued excitedly amongst themselves, then laughed, threw their weapons down into the canoe, and made signs of peace.

"Steady, boys," said Mr Clare. "Don't betray any sign of fear. Better these savages than the sharks. We have no choice. They could stand off with the canoe and kill every one of us with arrows if they wanted to. Do nothing to startle them and we may make friends."

The savages beckoned them to come aboard. The four lads felt a bit white. No one moved. At last Tommy Cheng the midshipman waded to the canoe: "At least there's a chance of reaching England in this," he smiled. "There's none in the raft."

"I'll chance it too," said big Bill Jeffrey, "It mightn't be as bad as it looks—so long as I don't have to kiss Flatnose."

Weakly the castaways followed him and tumbled down amongst the grisly weapons in the bottom of the canoe.

"They smell a bit high," grinned Bill Williams, "but beggars can't be choosers."

"Any perfume smells sweet to me after that raft," said Mr Mayer the second mate. "But never mind the smell. Keep your weather eye skinned; we might have to fight and take this canoe. What do you say, Mr Clare?"

"Not the faintest chance. Do nothing to annoy them. Should they turn on us, however, every man must snatch a weapon and do the best he can."

The savages, exclaiming "Toree! Toree!" eagerly splashed down on to the raft and snatched for the poles. With delight they examined the knives, while the disappointed ones reached under water at the planks, searching as eagerly as we would search for gold. They were seeking scraps of iron, the "Toree" which to them was far more valuable than gold. But except for the few knives lashed to the poles there was no more iron. Scowling their disappointment they climbed back into the canoe while the lucky ones showed their prizes as a child would a toy.

In spite of their fear the boys could not help admiring this large canoe, burned and chopped out from a tree-trunk. At intervals through its gunwales neat holes had been burned and through these stout poles stretched out fourteen feet from the side. To these was attached a long, neatly shaped log like an aeroplane float, but much longer. This was the outrigger. This balanced the canoe and allowed it to cruise through rough weather without capsizing. The outrigger supports and struts were stoutly lashed with rattan Vine.

To a hoarse growl from Cut-cut the savages sprang to it. Swiftly the canoe went about, swiftly sailed away. Expert seamen these.

Jack crouched beside John with muscular black bodies pressed all around them, while others squatted out on the outrigger for room.

Gutturally they spoke, with frowning, questioning faces discussing the two elder boys. The big chief and Biskea were vigorously convincing the other savages, pointing towards the boys with exclamations of "Wak!" "Kabi!"

Jack in surprise began to realize that they imagined they had met him and Sexton before.

"Seem to be old friends of yours," grinned Bill Williams. "I wish you'd give us an introduction."

"They're stupid," said John in bewilderment.

"Play up to them, boys" advised Mr Clare earnestly. "There may be something in this. Make friends with them whatever you do."

"If only for the sake of something to eat, Wak," murmured Tommy Cheng. The two little midshipmen were nearly done.

Suddenly grim black faces were peering into Jack's. A hand gripped his hair and jerked his head this side, then that while they gutturally exclaimed: "Wak! Wak!" They examined John Sexton similarly and called him Kabi, then squatted back, frowning at the boys, scratching their matted hair, arguing and puzzling.

"The lads seem to be their long-dead nephews or something." ... "I wouldn't care to call the big chief uncle." ... "I'd prefer him to Flatnose" ... were comments that followed in quick succession.

"That yellow circle around their eyes gives me the creeps," said Will Perry suddenly.

"Which way are we sailing, Mr Clare?" asked Will Hill.

"Nor'-west!" answered the mate. All sighed with relief. Mer lay nor'-east. They began to talk, to crack a joke now and then.

That afternoon they drew close to a small, dreary, low-lying island. The savages pointed and exclaimed "Boydong!" and grinned at them. They stared as a few wind-blown trees took shape, then patches of drab green bushes, then tufts of coarse grass rising above vines which trailed over sand-mounds.

"Boydong" is one of a group of islets that lies fairly close to Halfway Island, a little south of Orford Bay, towards the northern end of Cape York Peninsula. Savages appeared on the tiny beach. The warriors in the canoe arose and sent up a shout.

"Lamars!"

"Lamars! Lamars! Lamars!" echoed back from the beach to a flourishing of clubs, a waving of spears.

Jack's blood turned chill; John and the midshipmen looked a bit white. Jack was soon to learn that Lamars meant spirits, living people returned to earth life from the dead. All these savages believed that white people were spirits and would cause them harm if not quickly killed.

As the canoe grounded on the beach it was surrounded by infuriated savages. The castaways clustered together, determined to go down fighting, feeling that all was lost. Cut-cut leaped out, shouting violently and quietened his threatening henchmen. Then grinned towards the captives, pointing to Jack and John.

"Wak!" he exclaimed triumphantly. "Kabi!"

Silence fell as newcomers peered at the boys. Then low, excited exclamations broke out.

The mate stepped up to the big chief, smiled, touched him in friendly fashion, and made signs for water and food. After heatedly arguing the savages turned grinning to the prisoners and beckoned them to follow. In among the stunted casuarina-trees were heaps of ashes near rows of cooking stones. Well gnawed bones lay about. Here and there were mounds of hot sand that marked native cooking-ovens. The castaways glanced apprehensively at one another but were beckoned to sit down. Water in coconut shells was brought to them. They drank, greedily, gratefully. Then as women scraped the sand from an oven, they sniffed eagerly to the smell of freshly roasting turtle. They ate as only famished men can eat; they drank again. At last, one by one they lay back upon the sand. Sunset was merging into evening.

"That was good," sighed big Bill Jeffrey, 'the best meal I ever ate—if I never eat again. What do you think of our chances, Mr Clare?"

"An even chance," answered the mate cautiously. "All stick together and do nothing to upset them. I'm going to try and explain to the chief that it will pay him to hold us to ransom until some passing ship comes along. If I can only convince him, we will be saved. All savages in these seas are eager to trade, seeking iron for their weapons. I'll try and explain to the chief that a ship would give much, iron, if we are delivered up unharmed."

"That's right," nodded Jack Caen encouragingly. "I hope you can get him to understand, Mr Clare."

"I'm sure I can," answered the mate. "But don't all fall to sleep together—some of us must sleep with one eye open."

But the men were utterly exhausted. Darkness had come; peace was upon the sea. Soon nearly all the castaways lay asleep.

Jack Ireland leaped up to sudden screams, thud of clubs, grunts of desperately fighting men.

"John! John!" he shouted and saw poor little Will Perry clubbed, then little Cheng and Mr Mayer went down fighting. Then the giant chief rushed him; he dodged the club blow and snatched aside the spear that grazed his side. Hurled to the ground, he grasped a sinewy wrist and wriggled up again fighting for his life, glaring at the eyes of that maniacal face. The infuriated savage struggled to cut his throat, but Jack grasped the blade and felt his fingers cut to the bone. Cut-cut, who had killed many men, was staggered at the fight this boy put up. He threw him down again and jabbed his knee in his chest. But Jack clung to the dagger, and wrenching over, leaped up and raced for the sea.

As he ran he saw John thrown down with Biskea at his throat; saw John sink his teeth into the savage's dagger arm; saw Mr Clare running towards the canoe; saw him overtaken and killed. Jack dashed into the sea and tried to swim out, then sobbing, turned wearily back to the beach. His heart was thumping frantically, his head buzzing; the sting of the salt water pained his wounds; he felt he was bleeding to death. The sea meant certain death. The shore meant...?

3

IN THE HANDS OF THE SKULL-HUNTERS

As Jack waded weakly ashore, Cut-cut leaped up from a victim and came bounding towards him, fitting an arrow to his bow. He loosed the arrow and Jack felt the sting through his shoulder. He collapsed, expecting death; but Cut-cut's face changed to pained concern and, grasping the arrow, he snapped it, then wrenched the protruding arrow-head from the wound. Jack fainted. Cut-cut carried, him to the trees and poured water down his throat. Through pain-dimmed eyes Jack, to his utter amazement, saw Biskea treating John Sexton similarly. The boys were left to their wounds and misery while the howling savages cut off the heads of the murdered men. Fires gleamed, then flames leaped up. The savages stacked the heads between the fires and danced around them until daylight.'

"Are there any more of us left?" whispered Jack.

"Not one."

"I saw that flat-nosed beast killing you. Why did he spare you?"

"I don't know."

"Are you badly wounded?"

"I feel terrible now, numb and burning all over. I can't move my hand, my side feels all torn away. But I can't feel any bones broken. Are you badly hurt?"

"Not nearly so much as you; Flatnose did not like my teeth in his arm, and in the scrimmage I managed to hide until it was nearly all over. I've only got this gash on my face and a broken rib, I think."

The boys huddled there, listening to those howls out by the firelight. Of all on that raft, only Jack Ireland and John Sexton were spared. And that was because the savages believed these two Lamars were sons of islanders they knew. And the savages were saving them to ransom them back to their supposed parents.

As this story and every incident written of in these pages, even to the wounds of the boys, is strictly true, I must explain that the chief Cut-cut would have killed Jack in the first mad rush, as Biskea would have killed John. When in fury, these savages think of nothing but to kill, kill, kill. After the killing was over the savage temperament cooled down. Then both Cut-cut and Biskea realized they had come very close to killing the two boys, and so losing a rich ransom.

Remember, Jack Ireland and John Sexton were living boys. Cut-cut was the actual living chief of the Aureed Island skull-hunters, and Biskea was his leading man.

Early next morning the savages collected all the heads, then signed to the boys to embark. They crawled aboard, Jack weak and ill from shock and loss of blood. The canoe sailed swiftly among a chain of small islands. Some were rocky and barren, others sandy and wind blown, with drooping casuarina-trees, tufts of. coarse grasses, and patches of vine scrub. Others again were hedged by thick fringes of mangroves. In plain view now was the wild Australian coast with its grim ranges, dark with scrub and forest. They were sailing up along it, drawing near the top of Cape York Peninsula, where at Peak Point (the most northerly point in Australia), it runs out into Torres Strait. Presently the canoe began to draw off towards the north-east. At sunset they landed on Pullan Island and were greeted by an excited crowd of savage men, women, and children. Loudly these acclaimed the victors who, flourishing the heads and weapons, strode towards a group of huts.

Jack clutched John as George D'Oyly stared towards them. And there was Will D'Oyly crying in the arms of a native woman. A loud bark, and old Portland came bounding towards them. Jack flinched, with wagging tail the dog jumped up to his wounded side. John patted Portland away from Jack, who gazed around in hopeful joy. Sexton squeezed his arm and nodded—from gaunt poles above the huts stared the heads of their other shipmates. Jack felt sick.

They sat down beside George D'Oyly.

"Were any saved?" asked Jack.

"Only Willy and me," sighed George. "They snatched Willy from mother's arms." He began to sob. A warm muzzle licked Jack's wounded hand.

"Poor old Portland!" he whispered.

"Yes," said George dully, "he sprang at their throats when they attacked us. But they clubbed him —not so hard as the others."

Wild youngsters, flourishing small spears, crowded around them. The whites of their eyes were rolling as scornfully they prodded the boys—to leap back as Portland snarled towards them. Young Will cried to come to them, and presently the native woman set him down. He ran to Jack Ireland.

The savages were grouped together, in excited talk and laughter, recounting the adventures of the last few days. The wild-eyed women were busy preparing a feast. The boys, huddled together, presently heard them at the feast; and from feverish sleep awoke to the sound of harsh laughter throughout the night. Several women threw them some cooked fish, but gave more to Portland than to the boys.

Next morning Jack could not move his arm and shoulder, and his side was raw and feverish. John's wound was badly inflamed. The woman who was looking after Will D'Oyly drew attention to their plight. The savages only laughed. She protested shrilly, and presently Cut-cut and Biskea came frowning towards them, carrying a coco-nut full of dugong oil. Roughly they salved the wounds, laughing at the flinching of the victims. It was not mercy that made them treat the boys, it was fear that the captives might die and they would lose the ransom. Angrily they gesticulated towards the oil and wounds, then strode away.

"We've got to look after ourselves," gasped John. "We'll boil water presently in one of those cooking-shells and bathe the wounds; we must keep the flies away somehow. But that oil *does* soothe, it takes away the burning."

During the next two months the four boys cruised with the savages, sailing from island to island, from reef to reef. For this was the fishing-season and these men were far from their home, following the great shoals of fish that constantly travel from feeding-ground to feeding-ground throughout the Coral Sea at this season of the year. Happily the weather was pleasantly warm, for the boys' clothes were rags now. In only a matter of days they learned to make their own fire, to scoop holes in the sand in which to sleep warmly, to make a breakwind, to cook their own food. Quickly they began to pick up the native language, to learn that they were travelling with men of Aureed under the great chief Cut-cut. They soon found that to disobey him would possibly mean death, even to one of his own warriors.

As day by day Jack saw new feats of this man's great strength and witnessed scenes of ferocity, he wondered again and again how he had managed to escape him on that terrible day. He felt he could never do so again.

Fish-spears were thrust into their hands; roughly they were told to make their own in future, to fend for themselves, or starve. As an indignity they had to help the women gather the wongai, the bright purple plums massed on dull green trees, and prowl the reefs, seeking shellfish. The young woman looking after young Will D'Oyly took pity on them and taught them to guard against shellfish which were poisonous.

They bucked up when they visited an island where the trees looked like snow from the masses of Torres Strait pigeons. Plump birds, sweet eating. All were thankful for Jack's foresight in not making enemies of the savage lads; for, now, the lads delighted in showing the Lamars how to shoot the pigeons with bows and arrows. Many a good meal of roasted pigeons the crowd of savage children and the four lonely white boys enjoyed under the wongai-trees close by the crooning sea.

The boys' wounds healed rapidly. They grew very brown as they regained strength, their misery gradually forgotten in this wild life, in the stress of every day fishing and hunting.

"If it wasn't for the memory of all our shipmates," sighed John Sexton one day, "and the occasional cold nights, I would love this life. It is wonderful."

"Yes," said Jack, as patiently he hardened the prongs of a fish-spear in the ashes, "we call ourselves civilized, but what a lot we must learn when we have to live as savages."

"It's different to going to a comer shop and buying food", laughed John. "This having to make a spear and go and find food for yourself makes you think a lot."

"I never thought we could live without money," said Jack.

"I never even think of it now," laughed John. "What a lot of things we forget when we don't feel the need of them! But what will be do without clothes when the rainy season comes?"

"These savages do without clothes all the year round," said Jack, "and what they can do we can. We've managed very well so far anyway. We'll have to watch what they do, that's all. But it's George I'm most sorry for."

They glanced out along the reef at George D'Oyly, trying to gouge a clam from its shell with a splintered bone as a knife.

"Young Will is almost happy," said John. "He has made mates with the young children, and the women have grown fond of him."

"He is fortunate to be only a baby. But he cries for his mother during the night-time. If only they don't kill him before help comes!"

John Sexton glanced around. No one was on the beach but themselves.

"You know no help can possibly come," he said; "our only hope lies in ourselves. Let us learn all we can: the fish, the tides, the bird-life, the finding of fresh water, the reefs, the handling of a canoe. Then, some night, load the swiftest canoe with spears and turtle meat and water, and the four of us sail south on a strong tide."

"S'sh!" whispered Jack, "even the bushes might hear." He bent down and patted the dog. "Of course Portland will come with us," he smiled.

Several months later the canoes sailed for Aureed Island, the savages elated at going home. Cut-cut stood in the bows with all the pride of a victorious chief. On his mighty figure even the warriors gazed with awe. Happy cries broke out as Aureed hove in sight. The boys gazed eagerly as graceful palms appeared above the sea; this island looked fairer than any island they had yet seen. The boys wondered what might be in store for them here but were not afraid, for they now knew they were to be held for ransom.

As the canoes drew close, people thronged the shore and a loud halloing broke out. The savages landed with much ceremony. Then, amid a sudden quietness, Cut-cut took the lead, and all marched inland.

Along an avenue of whispering palms stretched a broad path bordered with large stones and giant shells, painted in red ochre. Here and there stood a pole, from which waved charms in the form of feathers, strings of shells, and painted ribbons of coco-nut leaf. At the end of the avenue stood a large, palm-thatched hut, with a black Zogo-stone before it. Tall bamboo poles with cross sticks adorned with grisly ornaments stood at the corners of this sombre building. This was the Zogo-house, and fronting it waited the Zogo-man—a terrifying figure, hidden behind a huge mask ghastly with rows of sharks' and dogs' teeth, and saucer-shaped eyes of gleaming pearl-shell. Tufts of brilliant feathers and bands of cowrie shells and crabs' claws adorned his painted arms. His legs were partly hidden behind a silvery petticoat of zim leaves. Behind that fearsome mask Jack sensed the Zogo's eyes gleaming evilly. Each movement of this grotesque figure was echoed by the boom of a drum, and a shrill of rattles from deep within the Zogo-house.

Within that gloomy place was the Au-guid, a giant figure carved like the squatting figure of a man. It was made of picked plates of polished tortoise-shell. Its face was enormous, with a queer, sneering expression. From the ears, there stood out all around the head a weirdly shaped hood of tortoise-shell, ornamented with coloured cowrie shells. Around this horrid figure hung many painted skulls—of victims slain in head-hunting raids. Now, with impressive ceremony new skulls joined them.

The boys stood with bowed heads, apparently seeing nothing, hearing nothing, as the deep chanting droned on. John stood side by side with George D'Oyly, Jack protectingly held his arm around the little brother. Glad were they when it was all over.

After several days of ceremonies all embarked for Sirreb Island, near by. This was the headquarters of the skull-hunters. Aureed was their sacred island, sacred to their beliefs and to Zogo.

Time went by. The boys met many more people here, for this was a gathering of the clans of the skull-hunters. They saw that Cut-cut was the big chief of many clans. They now understood the language and could fend for themselves, for this was still the delightful season of the year. They had yet to learn what it meant to battle for a living during the rainy season.

Now they could hunt for themselves, whether for fish or birds, edible fruits or yams, shellfish or other life from the reefs, sandbanks, and mudflats. They had adapted themselves to life aboard canoe, learned to read the signs of life ashore , and at sea, and to handle native weapons. They knew where to look for and light a fire by rubbing certain dry sticks together; knew just where to search for' water whether on ocean beach, in scrub, or sandhill. They knew the right wood to select for a spear-haft, and the hardwood for the spear-head; knew how to obtain and treat the gum, and how to make the fibre string which glued and bound the head to the haft. These and many things they simply had to learn, in -order to live.

Young Will D'Oyly had long since become such a favourite that he bullied the savage boys with impunity. And he could speak their language now almost as well as they. He answered to the name of Ewas. Jack was always called "Wak", John Sexton "Kabi", and George D'Oyly "Sagibi".

The boys were taken as a matter of course now and had lost most of their fear. But an unhappy day was coming.

4

RANSOMED

All was bustle for departure, women and children carrying aboard the long bamboos full of water, baskets full of wongais, yams, dried pigeons and fish. The crews were in joking mood as they collected their weapons. A bright day with the Coral Sea lazily blue; difficult then to believe that howling cyclones ever sweep across this beautiful sea. Cut-cut, waving his club and roaring a war-song, marched down to the canoes. Biskea and the savage warriors gay in fresh paints and feathers followed, climbing aboard the canoe and calling to the boys.

They were to be separated. George D'Oyly clung to young Will, Jack and John stood unhappily by. Old Portland gazed from puzzled brown eyes, half-heartedly wagging his tail. To an angry roar from Cut-cut George whispered brokenly: "Look after him, Jack. Good-bye", and turned and walked hurriedly to Mal-goor's canoe.

Jack put his arms around the sobbing baby boy, and held out his hand to John.

"We're certain to meet again," John said.

"Of course. Look after yourself, John."

"Sure I will," answered John and hurried after George.

Portland stood there indecisively until a savage snarled to him to jump overboard. He whined; ran to Sexton; ran back to young D'Oyly; then stood shivering. A native picked him up and walked away; but he bit the man, who then took him by the throat, shook him furiously and flung him into a canoe.

The canoes were pushed off and all jumped aboard. To a rollicking sea-song the sails were hauled up and the canoes stood away from Aureed, swiftly drawing apart.

Jack and Will gazed after their mates in the vanishing canoe, waving until Portland's frantic barks came to them faintly, and the canoes were out of sight. Jack wondered whether he would ever see John Sexton and George D'Oyly again.

He never did.

The savages cruised from island to island, staying just as long as the good fishing and hunting lasted. A few days here, a few days there, a month on the fruitful island. Such an island would grow wild fruit and yams, and be surrounded by a coral reef, the feeding-ground of numerous fish. Jack noticed that from island to island they were sailing north-east.

One afternoon by far the largest island he had yet seen loomed up.

"Eroob!" laughed the savages as the hills and dales and palm groves of that lovely island rose higher from the sea.

As the canoe skimmed towards Medigee Bay Jack stared at stone walls stretching out into the sea. This was the Great Sai—acres of stone-walled fish-traps.

Under the palms of Eroob a great concourse of people awaited them near a large village of beehive shaped huts. These islanders were evidently much more advanced in culture than the Aureed skull-hunters. Their weapons, their strongly built villages, their large gardens, the neatly made and prettily-dyed grass skirts of the women, the beautiful head-dresses of the warriors proved these people to have advanced far above nomadic tribes. The war canoes fairly took his breath away. One enormous vessel he thought must be a hundred feet long. When he stood in it, his head only just appeared above the gunwale. The manner and independent bearing of these people proved them far superior to their present visitors.

Surrounded by a great crowd of people, Jack and Will were closely examined. Jack saw the tense excitement, noticed the half-triumphant, half-snarling expression on Cut-cut's face, the uneasy grin on the savage countenance of Biskea. The fate of the two boys was at stake. Jack realized their heads might yet decorate the canoe of Cut-cut.

At last the big Mamoose, the leading chief of all Eroob, stood back to give his verdict. Jack gazed from anxious eyes as the deep-toned voice rolled out. Voices broke in with delight, greeting the verdict with the greatest pleasure. Men, women, and boys thronged around Jack and Will calling them Wak and Ewas as if they had known them all their lives.

Cut-cut and Biskea stood back grinning, very pleased with themselves, sure of the ransom now.

From that time on Jack and Will were treated with every kindness. A fortnight later, on a brilliant sunlit morning the Mamoose took Jack up the big hill Lalour, and pointed far away. Jack saw a blur of greyish-blue, which experience told him was a large, wooded island.

"Mer!" smiled the Mamoose. "From there, when the winds allow, your father Duppa will sail and ransom you from the savages, the skull-hunters of Aureed. Fear not, for now we have guaranteed you."

Jack understood, although this pleasant language differed from that of the savages. He was to go to Mer, the Mer that all the men of the *Charles Eaton* had feared so. But these islanders of Eroob were friends of Mer and had treated Will D'Oyly and himself very kindly. He wished they could stay on Eroob, and see the last of Cut-cut for ever. But they were forced to embark again with the savages and return to Sirreb Island. Jack stared unhappily towards grim Aureed.

A fortnight later a war canoe swiftly approached Sirreb. It was massed with warriors, its flag of peace (a shredded palm branch) waved from the top of each mast. It came swiftly under two broad mat sails. Stretching across the canoe nearly amidships like a ship's bridge, right to the double outriggers was the fighting platform, now crowded with warriors whose plumes were ablaze with colour. Its tall prow and taller stem were gaudily decorated with feathers and gaily coloured shells. To perfect seamanship as it skimmed right up on the beach down tumbled the big sails, out leaped the warriors.

Better looking, more powerful, except for the giant Cut-cut, more tastefully decorated than the savages, were these well-armed men. Their thick hair fell around their shoulders in ringlets. Some were bearded, some clean shaven. Some were of a dark brown complexion with flashing eyes and attractive laugh, active movements and an expression of cocksure certainty. These were men not to be trifled with; men very sure of themselves—men of Mer.

The warriors stood by the canoe while a tall, elderly warrior came running towards the two white lads. He knelt by Will, looking intently' into his face. Then cried "Ewas! Ewas!" and flung his arms around Will and cried. Jack knew this must be Duppa who had accepted Will D'Oyly as his son. Surely he would not make the same mistake with Jack Ireland!

Jack glanced at Cut-cut. The giant was standing with folded arms, a grin from ear to ear. If Duppa did not accept Jack Ireland as his son then Cut-cut in his disappointment and rage would club Jack on the spot.

The old warrior sprang up, seized Jack eagerly and stared into his face. Then thumped him on the shoulder with a rollicking laugh, crying "Wak! Wak!" He flung Will on his shoulder and ran towards his warriors. They ran to meet him, laughing and singing.

Duppa of Mer was happy. He firmly believed that to him had been miraculously returned his own dear sons, who had been blown to sea in their fishing-canoe and drowned twelve months before. To a wave of his arm his warriors paid over the ransom and a feast was prepared.

On a distant island, young Sexton and George D'Oyly were being greeted similarly by two warriors, who also recognized these two boys as their sons.

Several days later the war canoe set sail for Eroob, for Eroob was allied to Mer and the Zogo-le of Mer had given Duppa messages to deliver to the Zogo of Eroob. They were received as friends and honoured guests at Eroob. Duppa sat all night in council with the Zogo-le. Then, his business concluded, hastened to sail for Mer, being anxious to deliver the two boys to their "mother".

"The old mother is dying to greet you, Wak", he said to Jack. "She nearly broke her heart when you and little Ewas were blown away. And ever since we received word that that big cut-throat had taken you from the Lamars, she has hardly slept a wink."

Poor Jack wondered whether it could be really possible that the mother would be deceived too. What would happen if she saw that these two boys were not her sons? Fervently he hoped she would be self-deceived too, if only for Will D'Oyly's sake.

Next day Mer loomed up, a large island of pretty hills rising steeply from the sea. Jack stared as smilingly Duppa pointed:

"Mer!" he said proudly. "The home of the Miriam-le, Chief. Lodge of the Zogo-le, rulers of all the Eastern Islands. And," he chuckled, "although they do not realize it, of all the Strait. And there rises old Gelam! high above the Zogo-house."

Jack saw the big crown that was the crater of the old extinct volcano Gelam.

"Gelam!" repeated Duppa in a deep soft voice. "It is Gelam our babies first see when the mothers hold them up in their arms. Gelam is the last that our warriors see when we sail from Mer; and the first we see when we return. And Gelam is the last we strive to see when we pass to Boigu, Isle of the Blest." Rapidly the lovely island appeared nearer, its miles of shores massed densely with groves of coco-nut palms, its pretty hillsides grass covered, darker patches of jungle and scrub here and there.

"The Sail," pointed Duppa. "You know it well, boy; from there it was you and young Ewas were blown to sea by the cyclone. Not so large as the Great Sai of Eroob, for our shores are not so suitable for its building. A big Sai all the same, and it traps many fish. But won't Pamoy be waiting to see you! She will be gazing out from Gelam-Pit now."

"I may have changed so much," said Jack doubtfully, "that she may not recognize me."

Duppa laughed.

"Did not the men of Aureed recognize you?" he cried. "And the people of Eroob? And I and my warriors? You have not changed, Wak, not in the least, except that you have grown a little taller and stronger, as is natural. You are whiter because you are a Lamar. Only that little Ewas is white he has not changed. All the world would know him."

Jack glanced towards young Will—really Ewas now, happy and laughing in the crook of Duppa's strong right arm. They were sailing close in to the Sai, the warriors singing as the canoe sped close in towards

Mer. Crowds of people were streaming down to the beach. Under the palms along the shores nestled villages, heavily stockaded. They swept past many canoes, then sped far up the beach to a shout from the crowd hastening to meet them. Duppa jumped ashore with Will in his arms, calling "Ewas! Ewas!"

A native woman ran towards him crying, with her arms held out. She snatched Will from Duppa and covered his face with kisses crying: "Ewas! Ewas!"

Jack felt left out in the cold. He looked around at excited islanders, at the village under the palms, secure behind its tall stockade, at the fleet of huge war canoes drawn up on the beach. Monster carved and painted beauties; several would hold a hundred men. And what men! Warriors black and dark brown with the chiefs flaunting head-dresses vivid with bird of paradise plumes.

People came hurrying to Jack. Old Pamoy threw her arms around him, the tears streaming down her face; Then she turned again to fondle little Ewas. Easy to see who had been the favourite of Duppa's sons.

A giant savage held up his arm. Jack knew by the magnificent head-dress, the triple row of sharks' teeth around the neck, the glittering ornaments of carved pearl-shell adorning his muscular limbs that he was the Mamoose, the chief of chiefs.

Instant silence fell on the crowd. In a deep voice that rolled out over the bay the Mamoose told how Duppa's sons had been recovered as Lamars from the sea. He declared that this was a time of rejoicing for all Mer; and decreed that every village must pay tribute of vegetables and fruit, of dugong and turtle, and congregate at the feast fires of the Big Village for rejoicing.

5

JACK MAKES A FRIEND

Merrily the hundreds of people scattered along the beach and hill paths, making for their villages to collect tribute. It would take three days to get ready for the feast. Jack with Duppa and a crowd of people walked along the sea-shore, then up and down the rounded, grassy hills. Jack glanced at a little stone figure smiling from a coral shrine beside the track; a quaint figure of carved stone with large white shells and painted stones around him.

"I see you remember Kaba Zogo," smiled Duppa. "But come, you will soon renew friendship again with them all."

They walked on past the villages of Keweid and Serwaged with here and there along the path tall bamboo poles, from which floated ribbon-like strips of palm leaves, teased coco-nut fibre, feathers, and strings of small, tinkling shells. These were various charms to flower or fruit or bird.

Jack was to learn that all over the island in pretty spots were little carved figures representing seasons or dugong or fish, vegetable or fruit, wind or rain. Through the Zogo-le these figures pleaded to the rulers of the seasons, fishes, birds, fruit, etc., for good seasons for the humans. Thus the Zogo-le held still further influence over the superstitious minds of the islanders.

At last they came to Las. Through the tall stockade, past the armed guards, they entered the village. A lovely village crowned with palms, overlooking the grim isles of Dauar and Waiar. From the jagged battlements of Waiar rose a still, thin column of smoke. Jack shivered, for it looked an evil isle. And it was.

Las was a village of many houses, built high above the ground, and shaped like enormous beehives. Neatly thatched with strips of seasoned palm leaves, the domed roofs were proof against the weather. By each entrance-way rested giant white clam-shells, containing water. Fishing lines, nets made from fibre string, fish-traps of plaited cane shaped like barrels, harpoons and paddles, weapons and garden tools and cooking pots were scattered among the huts.

There were very few dogs. Jack had long since learned that dogs were of little use to island people.

By each warrior's house was a tall pole, the Sarokag pole. Some were adorned with skulls; some with other reminders of the warriors' fortune in battle. (A hut without a Sarokag pole belonged to a man not a warrior.)

And at the entrance to each house waved a Lamar charm, a charm to keep out unwanted spirits.

Duppa's large hut stood in the centre of the village. Cheerily the people escorted them to it while Marboo the big chief of Las placed his hand in friendly fashion on Jack's shoulder.

"Welcome back to Las," he said in the pleasant tongue of the Miriam-le. "We will give thanks to the Zogo-man that he may thank the Great Zogo for your safe return."

A fearless looking lad stood beside Marboo, curiously watching Jack. This lad was Bogo, the chief's son. He and Jack were destined to share many adventures together.

Jack knelt and followed Duppa through a tiny doorway. Then stood upright—and caught his breath. Two great eyes gleamed from a frightful countenance, part of the shrivelled figure of what had been a man. The figure glaring down upon him stood stretched to bamboo poles.

"Duppa-Mer," said Duppa softly, and stood in reverence before the mummy. Jack shivered. That awful figure was supposed to be his grandfather. Every warrior's house in every village thus treasured its mummy, which guarded the home, unless he had been killed in battle far away. Jack soon became used to these figures, as he did to others stretched up on poles along certain of the. paths. The floor of the hut, raised well above the ground, was of neatly fitted laths of bamboo. Covering the floor was a mat tastefully made of plaited palm leaves. On this was Pamoy's mat, Duppa's mat, and two smaller mats. Pamoy was still fondling young Ewas, who was talking eagerly in the island tongue, very interested in his new home. Duppa pointed at the corner of the hut and smilingly said:

"See. Your mat still awaits you!"

Jack squatted native fashion, looking at the long spears of many patterns, the great war bow, the sheaf of arrows, the clubs of various kinds, the Doad with its terrible shafts, the long daggers of cassowary-bone placed handy along the wall. It must need all a man's strength to pull the bowstring of that bow, thought Jack.

"Yours are there too," said Duppa. "I have kept them oiled, awaiting you. They are just as you left them on that terrible day when the cyclone blew your canoe to sea."

Jack saw on the wall beside his mat a neat array of boy's weapons, beautifully made. He felt a sudden eagerness to try these weapons, so very different to the crude things he and John Sexton had made when cruising with the savages. For some time he admired these weapons which were his very own, then his gaze wandered to the food-baskets and cooking-pots in Pamoy's comer of the hut, to the neat grass skirts made from the bark of the fig-tree root, teased fine as silk.

He was home. He wondered how long this hut, this village, this island would be home to him. Will D'Oyly (little Ewas) now had gone to sleep in Pamoy's arms. Jack was glad. He was determined to be Duppa's elder son in all things, to be all that Duppa thought him to be so that he might save Will D'Oyly and himself too. He would have to be very, very careful, to betray no alarm at anything, to learn the customs and language perfectly, to join in with the boys of his own age and become one of them as quickly as he could.

Young Will would be all right. He knew the language better than Jack; did not show alarm at terrible things; was happy to play with the children; was not afraid of the elders. Soon he would be a favourite.

Jack determined to become an islander of Mer— rescue must, come someday.

But that very evening a man came to Duppa's hut, an eager man with kindly face and eyes. Jack liked him until he realized that this man was going to be young Will D'Oyly's foster father. He had come to take him away.

Among these people (to this very day) there exists a universal custom of adoption. Many children are adopted. And on an occasion such as this, it is strict custom that one child shall be adopted—the younger. Oby was Duppa's friend, and Oby was to adopt Ewas.

Far into the night Duppa and Oby talked. Gravely they smoked the Zoob, a long pipe of bamboo, using yellow-leafed native tobacco. Pamoy was crying softly, crooning over young Ewas asleep on her lap.

It was decided that it would be best for Oby to take Ewas now, before he became too fond of Duppa's home. Later, when he had become used to Oby, he could visit Duppa and Pamoy very often.

It was after midnight when Oby gently took up the child and softly departed. Jack lay there, hearing Duppa sigh heavily and Pamoy crying to herself. But it proved a happy adoption. Ewas very soon grew to love Oby.

The next morning when Jack stepped out of the hut a lad was awaiting him—friend or enemy? Jack recognized him as Bogo, son of Marboo, the chief of Las. Bogo stood as tall as Jack and as strongly built, staring from fierce brown eyes. Jack gazed back. Then Bogo smiled and laid his hand on Jack's shoulder.

"Come," he said, "and we will help the people carry the food to Laid village. Marboo, my father the chief, orders that we be friends."

Jack smiled agreeably, they rubbed cheek to cheek, then turned towards the banana groves where men already were cutting bunches of bananas.

All that day men, women, and children carried down fruits to the village of Laid. From the hillside paths and along the shore people from other villages came with manioc and taro, yams and sugar-cane, turtle and turtle eggs, dugong meat and fish. Under the palms the women were digging the big cooking-ovens, heating the stones and spreading the meats on broad green banana leaves. These leaves would be wrapped around the meats, then all would be placed in the ovens. Fish and meats so cooked are clean, sweet and tender.

Children of all ages were eagerly helping, especially young Ewas staggering under his little load of bananas, calling merrily to the women, taking charge of the boys of his own age crowding after him. His bright eyes and quick little laugh were making him many friends. Jack was glad. Oby's smiling eyes never seemed to leave the child. Pamoy was watching, too, from a distance.

Bogo brought lads to Jack and introduced them. Jack, who long since naturally answered to the name of Wak, solemnly touched each lad's shoulder and murmured greeting. They were very curious about this Lamar, but all were friendly.

While all this activity was going on the bowmen never laid down their bows, the clubmen always carried their clubs, the spearmen their spears. Even the boys, introduced to him, carried bows and arrows. In their laughing and joking the warriors now and again cast a questioning glance out to sea. And on the island headlands there always stood a look-out man.

Jack was soon to learn that although Mer was a well-populated island of warlike men, it was constantly attacked by raiders from distant islands. Mer never really slept, either by night or day.

The drums beat first for a parade of young men and girls, prettily decorated in feathers and flowers and shells. Then all sat down to the grand feast which lasted for many hours with intervals of dancing by gaudily painted warriors and bands of flower-decked girls, whose wonderful black hair was gay with scarlet hibiscus. Smilingly proud were they of skirts of silken strands of fig-tree root. Competitions quickly followed in spear-throwing, club-swinging, and arrow-shooting.

Jack was fascinated by the bows and arrows, bows sometimes taller than a man and requiring great strength to bend. For hours he watched the long, vicious flight of the arrow travelling fast and true to its mark.

6

THE CHALLENGE

The men were drinking large quantities of a liquid brewed from coco-nut milk and fermented bananas. As they drank their songs grew noisier, their games more boisterous. And the women cheered them on. A young man proudly wearing the feathers of the Sea-hawk Clan drew a long, cruel dagger and flourished it. Laughingly he challenged a warrior of the Shark Clan. Instantly a ring was formed and the combatants crouched towards one another. Eyes gleaming, lips tight shut, clawing fingers seeking to snatch the dagger wrist of the other. Again and again they sprang to strike, only to twist in mid-air and bound aside, then instantly leap back to the fight.

A combatant would leap high, then was under his adversary, striking up, then was on his feet warding off a lightning blow. The Shark man twisted like an eel, warding as his dagger arm slipped under his adversary's guard to stab him in the back. Instantly they were at one another's throats, wrestling like madmen.

The Mamoose roared an order and warriors rushed in and, forcing the combatants apart, threw them back amongst their clansmen. To quell the excitement the Mamoose ordered a man of every clan to wrestle a man of another. Forty men leaped into the ring, crouching forward as they sprang to fall upon one another. Leaping back, they attacked again or, interlocked, sought to throw one another to the ground. Jack was fascinated by the wrestling match, so unlike the wrestling he had watched aboard the *Charles Eaton. This* was an all-in struggle to hurl an opponent down and throttle him. Expert club-fighters, yet not a blow was struck; these men knew nothing about fist-fighting but were terrible wrestlers.

Again the Mamoose stepped in and stopped the wrestling, for several fallen men were being strangled.

The people were now wildly excited. Lads of Jack's age rushed into the ring. These lads had recently been initiated from the Kwod (the training-school) and were eager to distinguish themselves. Bogo wheeled around and his excited laughter changed to an angry stare as he glared towards Jack. He leaped towards him, touched him lightly on the chest, then sprang back and called shrilly:

"I challenge Wak the Lamar, the son of Duppa!" All eyes were instantly on Jack. No one had expected him to be called for he had so lately, so they believed, returned from the dead. But it was a challenge!

Jack's heart beat fast; he knew he had no hope of wrestling this young tiger, though both were perfectly matched.

Bogo could and would choke him; Bogo's chest was heaving with excitement; excitement glared from the fierce eyes of the warriors as they waited. Jack felt Duppa's eyes upon him, proud eyes, eyes that grew troubled as he hesitated. He knew that he must fight Bogo. He stepped into the ring. There was a murmuring. The spectators were wondering how the Lamar lad would fight? He who must have forgotten nearly all he had learned.

Jack meant to fight, not wrestle. He was thinking swiftly, remembering the many friendly bouts he and John Sexton and the midshipmen had boxed on board the *Charles Eaton*; how the bosun and crew had encouraged them and taught them. But this might well prove a fight for life. Looking into Bogo's fierce eyes, he realized this was to be a fight until one or the other was utterly beaten. Warily he shaped up, he must never allow those clutching hands to fasten around his throat.

Bogo sprang and Jack swung and missed, then uppercut almost a breath too late, wrenching his twisted arm from Bogo's grasp. The strength in that grip made him clench his teeth. As Bogo sprang again Jack bent him double with a right to the heart, but Bogo crashed upon him and both went down as Jack flung out his legs and kicked Bogo's grip from his ankle. Both leaped to their feet, Bogo panting, Jack furiously anxious now to get in a blow. He lashed out and caught Bogo smack! on the nose. Bogo reeled back in amazement, he crouched there with blood pouring from his nose. Jack would have laughed had he dared. There arose one mighty "O-oh!" The people had never seen man or boy struck on the nose before. Jack heard little Ewas's cry of delight. The anxiety on Duppa's face changed to one big grin. All awaited eagerly; they had never seen a fight like this before.

Bogo advanced in bewildered fashion, his eyes rolling, his smarting nose dripping crimson. Bogo would have laughed and fought madly on to a wound from spear or dagger but he could not take a punch on the nose. He screamed and leaped forward, clawing for Jack's throat. They crashed down with Bogo on top, while Jack glared up into a fiendish face and felt thumbs of steel pressing around his throat. He punched over Bogo down upon his kidneys, punched fiercely while still he had strength. Bogo grunted at each blow and suddenly leaped up with agonized face, bent almost double. Jack was hurt too; he struggled for breath as he rose. Through a mist he stared towards Bogo. Painfully Bogo crouched forward, there was no springing forward now. In all his severe training in the Kwod never had he known wrestling like this, nor seen the warriors fight so. Warily he circled around Jack.

The people were thinking the one thing—that Duppa's son had brought with him a new way of fighting from the skies. In tense silence they waited. Jack manoeuvred threateningly while secretly getting his wind. If Bogo closed with him again he would never have another chance. He determined to punch Bogo one great blow below the ribs. Bogo could not take that blow on the nose or those thumps on the kidneys, what would he feel like if he stopped one fair in the wind?

Jack stepped in to leap back as Bogo suddenly bent his knee. Again and again Jack stepped in, shamming light blows to confuse Bogo. Gradually he fought as if growing tired; he saw Bogo's eyes light up, saw him about to spring again, then stepped in and swung with all his strength. Bogo grunted "Oooch!" doubled up with his hands to his stomach, and collapsed.

He lay there, squirming. Jack stood over him, frightened now. Then glanced across at Duppa.

Duppa stepped forward with a proud smile, and slapped Jack hard on the shoulder. Jack helped the gasping Bogo to his feet, consoling him all he could, very anxious to make friends. Bogo glared back from watery eyes, not knowing what to do. The people silently looked on, they had never seen such a fight as this, nor seen one end so. When Bogo could stand upright Jack showed him how to shape up, promised to teach him how to become a great fighter, much greater than he. Bogo smiled with a quick, painful pleasure. Jack laid his cheek to his, and Bogo responded.

A chorus of talking rose up as the people crowded around them, Marboo the chief stepped forward and smilingly laid his hand upon Jack's shoulder. Duppa laid his hand upon Bogo. They were friends. A roar of approval rose up as smilingly the Mamoose congratulated them. Excitedly talking over the strange fight, the people returned to the feast.

Jack had made a friend, and won the people's respect.

Next morning Bogo climbed into Duppa's house.

"Come!" he smiled. "The people will sleep the day away after the feast. Duty takes me to the Sai. Bring your fish-spear."

Eagerly Jack selected a three-pronged spear from the neat stack that Duppa had told him were his before he was "drowned". The boys hurried through the village, past the sleepy-eyed guards at the stockade entrance, then on to the winding path leading down to the sea. A light breeze waved the grass upon the hillsides, lovely birds sang sweetly from the dark patches of jungle, the sea was very blue. Bogo drew a deep breath.

"I love it," he said. "Mer and the sea are the world to me. You were a skilful hand in a canoe before you were blown to sea, you must love Mer too. But wait until you see my new canoe, the *Seagull.* She's a beauty."

"You can teach me to handle her," said Jack, "and to spear fish and turtle nearly as well as you. I am out of practice, you know."

"Yes. My father says that every Lamar child forgets nearly all he learned; he must even learn his own language again. But they very soon learn. I will teach you everything I know."

"And I will teach you how to fight in the Lamar way," promised Jack: "everything I know I'll teach you."

They smiled, lightly placed hands on shoulders and walked gaily down to the Sai.

Already many grown lads and fishermen whose duty it was to oversee the Sai were busy there, for the tide was rushing out and the fish were swimming frantically in the great traps, seeking to escape.

"Here is my father's Sai," pointed Bogo. "It stretches out to those two big coral niggerheads that mark the boundary of Duppa's traps. Ha! that is a big one! He will take your largest spear to get him; he's in your father's trap."

Jack looked at the big fish swimming, hemmed in by the walls of rock. Far out around the Sai were shouts and exultant laughter as lads and men speared the fish, cries of disdain as a thrower aimed for a fish and missed. The startled fish were darting hither and thither, and Jack saw that skill was needed to spear them.

Bogo stood up on the Sai wall, his eyes shining, tense watchfulness on his smiling face. Suddenly his spear arm swung back; poised like a bronzed statue, he swiftly threw. Straight and true the spear sped, then the haft leaned over and hissed through the water.

"Bravo!" laughed Jack as Bogo jumped down into the water and half plunged, half swam to catch that travelling haft. He snatched at it and with a quick movement held, it out of the water with a flapping fish impaled on its prongs. Wading to the Sai wall he, with a single movement, jerked the fish into a basket.

Jack knew from his experience among the Aureed savages that to spear a fish requires skill; to lift it from the water so that it does not flap off the prong again requires skill; and to throw it from the spear into the canoe, basket, or on a reef requires a knack only gained by constant practice. He watched a fish, waited his chance, threw and missed.

"A good throw," shouted Bogo as he plunged for the floating spear. "You just grazed his side but the fish twisted. Try again; aim just a little ahead of the next one."

Jack smiled. He could have speared that fish.

7

JACK LEARNS TO FIGHT AND WORK

Jack handled his spear lovingly. It was three pronged, perfectly balanced. The feel of it even more than its appearance told with what care it had been made. "Duppa must have been very fond of the real Wak," thought Jack, "to have made him such a perfect set of weapons."

The three long, tapering prongs of the larger fish-spear were of hardwood further hardened by slow roasting in ashes. The prong points, so fitted to the haft that they jutted outward, commanded a circle as wide as the body of a fair-sized fish. Jack could hardly imagine missing a fish with a weapon so skilfully proportioned. The prong ends were neatly and securely bound to the haft by strong, oiled thread twisted from hibiscus fibre, then set in hardened beeswax. The haft was just the right length, perfectly straight and gradually tapering to the end, strong yet light. It would travel true and swiftly, would float buoyantly and thus speedily tire an impaled fish. The weight of the spear-head exactly balanced the prongs and haft. The feel of it made Jack's hand tingle, the weapon seemed to wish to leap out and fly at a fish. Cheerily he glanced about, eager now to show what he could do.

And when he did he surprised Bogo.

The big Sai built out from the shores was walled off into many lanes and squares and oblongs and narrow twisting passages, a maze that baffled the fish once they swam into any portion of it. Wherever they swam they met other walls, other twisting lanes. The one hope of escape was when the tide turned and began to rush back to sea. Shortly afterwards escape was hopeless, for by then the walls would show above the water. When the tide came rushing in with its hungry fish the water rose above the Sai. The fish at quiet water then entered the Sai—and became lost.

The Sai itself was divided into many small traps, each owned by a warrior or fisherman. Not every man owned a share in the Great Sai. Those who did not, received their share of fish by barter. A man might not own a trap, but he might be a maker of good weapons which were in keen demand. He thus earned fish for himself and family by the sale of the weapons he made.

Jack was soon to spend hours watching Ramos make him his first canoe. That canoe would be fashioned from a special lightwood log traded all the way from distant New Guinea, and it was to cost Duppa half the produce from the garden for a year. An expensive little fishing-canoe.

No man could build so light, so swift a canoe as Ramos. His cunning hands fashioned lines in a canoe that helped it skim the waters like a bird. Although all the big canoes were bought ready made from the famous canoe-builders of New Guinea, it was Ramos of Mer who was eagerly sought after to make or improve the small fishing-canoes. Ramos owned neither a share in the Sai nor a garden, but his canoes brought him everything he wanted.

Certain men of the lesser classes among the dreaded Zogo-hood were skilled in the mummification of the dead. Thus they earned *their* living. Other men were carvers of shells, a delicate work of value in trade with New Guinea as well as with the island people themselves.

Other men traded the produce of their gardens; others were fighting men, the first to rush into battle to defend the island; others were rope-makers, using various fibres from barks of trees and creepers for different kinds of rope and string; others were expert thatchers and builders of huts that could defy the heaviest rain. Still others were the makers of fishing-nets, or mixers of paints for the ceremonies, or the makers of the magnificent head-dresses.

The Zogo-le, of course, were the few men "up above", they who guided the destinies of the people.

All had their share in the life of the island.

Some women were makers of mats so pretty and durable they were eagerly traded for; some were the makers of skirts of different kinds, patterns and colours; some, makers of cooking-pots that would not crack for years. Any article that man or woman wanted, but could not procure or make for themselves, they could trade for. Ail lived quite happily; all had sufficient time to spare, and yet plenty of duties to attend to. But while theirs was in general a happy, contented life they had their worries and troubles, like all humans. Also they lived ever on the alert, prepared to leap to arms at any moment. Otherwise they would have been wiped out of existence.

Jack was almost happy. This was a much more secure and contented life than the life he had led when with the Aureed skull-hunters. They were nomads. These were settled people. He wondered what fate had befallen John Sexton and George D'Oyly. Word came occasionally by visiting canoe that they were living on an island far to the west. He hoped they, too, had fallen among friends? Young Will D'Oyly (little Ewas) was perfectly happy, greatly loved now by his foster-father Oby. Oby lived in a village some distance away but often visited Las with young Ewas.

Jack was now trained systematically and soon learned to handle the hunting-spear, the harpoon, the war-spear and club, and to become a good shot with the bow and arrow. He very soon showed Bogo that he could handle the fish-spear. Bogo then taught him a hundred ways to seek fish, both in deep water and shallow, among the reefs, on mud-banks and sandbanks, among the mangroves, and in a hundred undreamed of places. It would require a large book indeed to tell all that the islanders know about fishes.

Jack was taught how to swing the Gubba-gubba, the disk-headed club, the star-headed, and pineapple-headed clubs. These club-heads of different shapes and weight and balance were made of stone and were used differently. But he could not gain the knack of the throwing-club—the short little stone club which, accurately thrown, crashes against an enemy's kidneys and paralyses him. He had to learn the uses of numerous weapons, for only by becoming familiar with them could he hope to dodge them should need arise.

That need assuredly would arise some time, Duppa impressed upon him. Jack did not mind being unable to handle the Doad, a dreadful weapon only used by skilled warriors. Nor could he dive or stay underwater as long as these island boys born to the sea. He tried very hard, for he was fascinated by the underwater life of the sea. It was a new world to him.

"Never mind," consoled Bogo. "You can shoot an arrow and throw a spear and handle a canoe almost as well as the best of us. You'll learn the other things quickly when we join the Young Warrior Clan. We all *have* to."

Bogo very quickly learned to use his fists as well as Jack, and then he turned instructor in wrestling. Jack was a grateful pupil, with the result that he learned all things very fast.

He knew the island thoroughly now, all the hills and villages and headland look outs, the gullies and beaches, the Zogo-shrines and taboo grounds—all except the dreaded area walling off the Zogo-house, and the forbidden Valley of Deaudapat. This desolate valley stretches back inland from the base of old Gelam the dead volcano. A dreadful valley, lifeless and forlorn; not a bush grows upon it, not a bird whistles there. It was believed to be the abode of the dead before they depart to the Blessed Isle of Boigu, far up in the heavens. The Dead Valley was forbidden to all but the Zogo-le.

"It's a beautiful morning," said Bogo one day, "a light breeze, the sea calm, the waters warn. A great day for turtle. We've got no other duties to do—what say we go turtle-hunting?"

"Right," agreed Jack, and collecting harpoon and spears, they hurried down to the *Seagull.* A beautiful little canoe, with mast and single outrigger which balanced the sail so, perfectly, it could turn about in almost its own length. The *Seagull* was known throughout the Eastern Islands as being the fastest canoe in the group. Proud as Bogo was of the *Seagull,* he was nearly as proud of his harpoon which was pointed with iron. Jack knew that harpoon head had been looted from some wrecked ship but painful memories forbade him ask particulars.

It was only a warrior, or the son of a chief, who would have his harpoon tipped with iron.

"It is a beauty," said Bogo lovingly, as he fingered the sharp point. "It will pierce the hardest shell of a turtle, the toughest hide of a dugong. It will cut through anything and never break or bend. I would give much when I am a warrior to have all my weapons tipped with this wonderful material of the Lamars."

"If a Lamar ship comes this way," promised Jack as they launched the canoe, "I'll get you plenty." "Oh, Wak, would you? I could never repay you if you did." Wistfully then he said: "But Lamar ships very, very seldom are sighted from Mer. If they are they sail far away into Spirit-land like the wings of a gull vanishing into the heavens. Very rarely, by false fires on the cliffs at night, we have been able to lure one on to the reef. My father, the chief Marboo, once lured a ship ashore. This is part of the iron. It was all divided up into little pieces, for it took hundreds of our men to kill the Lamars."

"They put up a fight then," said Jack as the canoe skimmed out to sea.

"Oh, a great fight, killing our men with terrible 'murder-sticks'. But the warriors attacked in the night while the waves were breaking over the ship, attacked on all sides with canoes alive with men. They leaped aboard like angry ants swarming an ant-hill and soon it was all over."

Bogo steered by paddle as the canoe slipped over the waves. With spray dashing on them, the boys laughed to the shriek of the gulls swooping overhead. Bogo steered outside the great reef to where on the sea-bottom was a waving expanse of sea-grass, a field under the sea. Upon this grass the turtle and dugong feed.

"We're well over the grass now," said Bogo. "See! there's chewed grass floating on the surface. Dugong are feeding below as well as turtle. We'll take in the sail, and paddle. Keep a sharp look out—at any moment a turtle may come up to breathe."

Jack paddled steadily while Bogo stood in the bows with his precious harpoon half poised, his keen eyes piercing far down into the water. The harpoon-head was a very short piece of sharp, barbed iron with a hole in the end, through which fitted .the harpoon rope. This iron end fitted loosely, yet not too loosely, into a socket in the end of the bamboo haft. When the harpoon was thrown, the head would pierce the prey while the loose haft fell away. The rope, perfectly made of seasoned hibiscus fibre, was neatly coiled in the canoe bow, the end fastened to an outrigger strut.

Jack, paddling noiselessly, was watching Bogo's hand which directed the steering by a slight signal this way, then that, slow or fast, stop or go ahead. Suddenly the hand signalled "Back paddle!" and Jack brought the canoe to a stop as Bogo's harpoon arm drew back.

A big, snake-like head broke the water, the broad, glistening back of a turtle followed with a splash and hiss as the creature expelled air then gaspingly drew it in.

Bogo threw with all his strength and leaped into the water shouting "Paddle! Quick!" The turtle with a great hiss half rose from the water as the harpoon buried deep into its shell, then its flappers splashed and it dived, the rope hissing out. Bogo had grabbed the floating harpoon-haft and snatched at the bow of the canoe swiftly coming upon him. With a laugh and a leap he was into the canoe and standing on the bow laughing excitedly:

"Paddle! Paddle until he takes the strain or the rope will snap. That's right! He's diving deep! He's a beauty! We'll be heroes in Las for bringing this load of meat. Ah, the rope is all out! Now he's taken the strain! Ease paddling a little bit; let him take the strain, but not too much lest the rope break."

Jack never took his eyes from Bogo's hand, steering instantly to its slightest wave that followed the underwater twisting of the turtle. The canoe leaped through the water, but its weight soon told on the labouring beast and—it must come up for air.

"Paddle!" shouted Bogo suddenly. Jack drove the canoe through the water almost on top of the turtle as its gasping head broke surface. It dived again, and Bogo laughed.

"Easy! Paddle easily; let him partly tow us again. He's our meat now!"

Again and again the turtle broke water but each time the canoe was on top of him, forcing him to dive again. Each dive was shorter and shorter. At last he came to the surface and stopped there floundering, gasping for air. Bogo dived and came up beside it, laughing as the huge flippers wildly beat the water.

In an instant he was astride the big shell, then with a sideways movement and mighty heave he had capsized under the turtle. The great thing lay there helpless, upside down, as Bogo reappeared laughing.

"He's a beauty!" cried Jack.

"The biggest I've seen this season," laughed Bogo with hand on the shell. "No canoe this season has brought in a prize like this. I'll wind the rope around his flippers, then we'll have to tow him to Mer, he's too big for us to get aboard the canoe."

They were two happy lads who towed their big prize to Mer to receive the acclamations of the people. A fine green turtle, nearly three hundredweight of delicious meat. He was cut up on the beach and volunteers carried him to Las. Marboo and Duppa smiled proudly.

The shell was of little use, but several days later the boys harpooned a tortoise-shell. Its meat was not nearly so good as that of the green turtle, and a poisonous part of it had to be cut away by a skilful man before any dared eat it. But from its beautiful mottled shell old Zargareb carved prized ornaments for warriors; his wife Nepa made combs for the pretty hair of the girls; Bogo made fish-hooks which he and Jack soon tried out on the reef.

They had strong lines which Ahkep, the maker of fisher lines fashioned from fibre chosen from seasoned bark of the hibiscus plant. This cord which Ahkep so craftily rolled and twisted between the palm of his hand and thigh, then oiled with dugong oil and dried, could hold all but very strong fish. And there were plenty of these as Jack found to his disgust when he lost hook after hook. He learned to make hooks from turtle-shell as well as Bogo; it was laborious work. But if he did not make them, he had to harpoon a dugong for its oil, with which to buy fishhooks from Tarka the maker of hooks; or else sell his labour to buy the oil which would buy the hooks.

No man in Las could make such crafty hooks as Tarka; no man in all Mer, so boasted the people of Las. But then every village had its hook-maker and each was jealous of their own.

The boys' hooks were clumsy compared to the hooks of Tarka. Their hooks lost many a fish. The hooks of Tarka but few. Poorly made hooks and lines, poorly fashioned weapons wielded by unskilled men, could cause hunger. In times of scarcity of fish the traps along the Sai would sometimes be empty of fish.

And Jack, like all others, knew that they must work constantly and work efficiently for their living, or else go hungry.

8

DOWN IN THE UNDERWATER WORLD

Jack loved to sail in the *Seagull* with Bogo, then dive deep down among the coral reefs out from the island. He would go deep down to fairy grottoes where amongst beautiful corals strange plant things, half animal, stretched dreamy tentacles towards him. To submarine gardens where vivid flowers stared at him —really stared, for some among these flowers were queer, living things that turned curiously towards any vibration in the water. The first time that Jack saw a lovely flower emerge on a long stalk from a mass of weird leaves, he was amazed, and just stared as Bogo glided beside him. Bogo grinned, and thrust his flattened hand towards the flower. It flinched as if hit by a squirt of water, its long stalk withdrew into the plant as the flower closed its petals and disappeared. Its dignity had been hurt.

Fish more brilliant than any parrot swam curiously around him. Their scales sometimes shone like living fire, or brilliant emeralds, or glowed like opals. Even the scales of common fish are much prettier on the living fish under water than they are upon a dead fish. Jack admired their eyes, luminous as pearls, alive with expression too, curious eyes, frightened eyes, timid eyes, scornful eyes, cruel eyes. Some fish had snub noses, and among these were inquisitive fish that would swim up to him and want to kiss him—or so it appeared. They really would have done so, had he not brushed them away. These are the fish that pearl-shell divers often see; they appear to be licking their lips as they swim up to the diver's helmet, peer in through his face glass, and gently butt their noses against the glass to smell what kind of a creature is inside.

But Jack knew nothing of pearl-shell divers and diving-suits. Day after day he swam down into palaces of living corals, amazed at the sea-tress and grasses, the waving ferns and green trellises pulsing with life, at huge, black and green and purple india-rubber looking things that were really partly animal, partly plant life. When he touched some of these they would squirt a coloured fluid at him; others would withdraw into a cranny in the coral.

For the first time he saw crabs quaintly swimming deep below, saw shapes like firemen's helmets slowly moving across the bottom or clinging like gigantic snails to the coral precipices.

Bogo patiently taught him to train himself to stay down longer and longer; taught him the long, slow breathing exercises that gradually expand the lungs until they can store up an undreamed of quantity of air; taught him how to slip from the canoe, gradually fill his lungs, then slip down feet first, turn in the water and with a few effortless strokes glide straight down.

When he could do that, go deeper and deeper, stay under longer and longer, Bogo taught him many underwater things by expressions of his eyes and face, by gestures, and by movements of his arms, legs, and body. Taught him how to glide, remain stationary, twist and turn, and move effortlessly. How to hold himself to the bottom whether to coral, rock, sand, gravel, sea-grass or other vegetable growth; how to hold his air and, when he must, how to release it only little by little. And then how to rise from great depth by only a few steady but certain movements, shooting to the surface while conserving his strength. When he had learned to do these and other things he found he could repeatedly go deep down all through the morning, could stay down longer, could explore farther and see many more marvels than he otherwise could have done.

Bogo also taught him how to handle a fish-spear deep under water; how to seek fish that hid in the coral crannies or among the plants and weeds and grasses, or that lay camouflaged on the gravels or dug into the soft, powder-like sand that sometimes strewed the bottom. Thus he learned a quite different way of spearing fish and eels and crabs, and many other things besides.

Jack looked forward now to the big cruising trips, when the village canoes or combinations of canoes and men from different villages would take the sea for a few weeks' cruise. The crews then lived on what they caught from day to day while cruising at sea or among the reefs and sandbanks and islands more or less friendly to Mer. Always there was danger, for when well away from Mer a fleet of allied enemies might be met with at any time. But this was all in the game.

Any such fishing-fleet that left Mer was always in charge of a chief in a war canoe; all other vessels were the ordinary large, swift, ocean-going fishing-canoes. Still, every man went armed, though not in full war paraphernalia, for their main object was the winning of great fish for. their flesh, skins, bones, and oil; and the loading of the canoes with shells desired for their utility, size, beauty, or trading value. For defence the canoes depended upon ceaseless vigilance, on the ability to ran for it if threatened by a superior force, and on their own ability to fight.

And now one such trip was organized for Las, Laid and Keweid villages and to the delight of Bogo and Jack both were chosen to go. No doubt Bogo pleaded with his father the chief to obtain the coveted permission for him and Wak. To a cheery send-off from the islanders the fishing-fleet sailed, Marboo's *War Chief* in the lead, followed by Duppa's *Sea Eagle.* Bogo was aboard the *War Chief,* Jack in the *Sea Eagle.* The well-manned canoes that followed were in line but spread out as the flotilla took the sea. Each canoe was manned by a handful of warriors, a crew of deep-sea fishermen, and a sprinkling of lads who, having passed through the, Kwod, were now receiving training in all that applied to the everyday life, the advancement, and the defence of Mer.

This was to be the last big fishing-cruise of the season, for the cyclone season would soon be due. And, though they did not know it, this cruise was to be made into song by the play actors of Mer.

The canoes skimmed along under sunlight that sparkled on dancing waves, under a clear blue sky, and with a fight breeze that kept taut the big mat sails. Drawn by sure knowledge, a shrieking flock of gulls followed the canoes; there would be pickings later on. That afternoon Gelam was a haze upon the sea when the look-out man shouted and all hands saw the sea streaked with foam. A shout arose; out whipped the paddles to speed the sails. Kingfish in shoal! Countless thousands of gleaming bodies cleaving the sea into foam. How the gulls shrieked, diving low as if gone mad in urging the canoes to hasten— hasten!

Long lines were dropped astern baited with native cloth and bright disks of pearl-shell which gleamed and spun while tearing along the surface away behind the canoes. Big fish were leaping high to plunge back amongst their fellows as men jumped up bending bows, poising long, strong spears. The canoes clove in amongst the shoal and Jack had a vision of countless long, gleaming blue bodies speeding over the surface, and just below it a picture of lithe movement and speed. He threw but the target had sped by. Only accomplished spearmen and bowmen could hit such speedy targets.

All men now shot and threw in tense silence, broken only by the grunt or hiss of the marksmen. As fish after fish was struck the spear-hafts went careering through the water, causing startled fishes to swerve aside or thump against the canoes. In the excitement Jack threw his spears and missed; the gulls hissed past the men's faces as they whirled shrieking into the melee.

A blue comet leaped from the sea, and to a terrific smack, Jack was knocked overboard among thousands of darting fish. He arose, gasping to the hiss of fish cleaving the water beside him. The *Sea Eagle* sped on to a howl of laughter. As Jack swam he saw another gleaming beauty leap clean between the masts of the *War Chief.* Jack had been fortunate. Had that speeding body struck him full on, it might have caused him serious injury, for there is great weight behind the big fish when they leap through the air like that.

The canoes followed the shoal until all the spears were thrown, then a shout of laughter went up, and arms pointed across the sea where spear-hafts were tearing through the water. Laughing voices came floating to Jack.

"Where is Wak?" he heard Samsu shouting. "Has any one seen Wak?" Jack felt sheepish.

The canoes came about as the stem-men hauled in the lines, each of which held a vigorously fighting fish. A hearty shout greeted the first fish aboard; it came in over the stem of the *Sea Eagle,* a fighting sixty-pounder thrashing about in the canoe. It was out paddles then and a scatter as the canoemen picked up floating spears and chased the bobbing hafts that marked hooked fish swimming in frantic circles, their white bellies gleaming as the weight of the long spear-hafts dragged them over and over.

Jack was still swimming, following the *Sea Eagle* as she circled again and again chasing this man's spear, then another's. At last all the fish and spears were recovered and the *Sea Eagle* turned towards Jack. Probably Duppa could have picked him up sooner but had left him to learn the lesson: "Always be wary. Anything might happen."

As Jack climbed aboard the others shouted: "The last fish comes! *What* a big one!"

Jack grinned, but resolved never to be "caught" like that again.

It had been a good haul. None of the boys had speared a fish, much to Bogo's disappointment. His first spear had impaled a fish but the frantic thing had broken loose and vanished. Still, all who had not won a fish had gained experience.

Sundown came; a sky of deepest blue was covered with drifting clouds like whitest fleece that turned to gold and rose as the sun sank down. The sea turned gold and softly changed into pink that merged into rippling silver. The deeper voices of the men rose and fell in the sweet canoe song of the Miriam-le. The fleet was approaching a coral atoll, a magic isle with its drooping palms throwing wonder shadows upon a golden beach. They skimmed over the reef into a coral lagoon and sped straight up on to the beach to a grinding of shell grit and sand.

All hands leaped out; each crew grasped its canoe and ran it up above high tide in a position from which they could rush it back into the water should alarm arise. Fish were thrown out, weapons stacked handy, the long bamboos full of drinking-water were lifted from the canoes, fires were started, fish made ready for the cooking. Each man set to, hungrily they squatted around the fires and ate.

Night came in velvet blue. Stars peeped out one by one, twinkling golden eyes. A laughing, silvery moon burnished the water into loveliness. Out on the reef little waves crooned lazily, but the lagoon was still as a polished mirror. A fish leaped up and fell with a plop.

Marboo the chief commenced a slow song in a deep, rich voice. The men of Las and Laid joined in the chorus. Jack had never known such a beautiful night. .

"Come!" said Bogo softly. Jack followed him to the beach. Little crabs scuttled before their feet, powdered shell and speckled sand gleamed like diamond pin-points. Bogo waded out, looking beautiful half bathed in moonlight and water.

"You love the wonders of the coral gardens," said Bogo softly. "We will visit them in moonlight."

He swam out to the centre of the lagoon and both lads trod water, slowly filling their lungs, drinking in air, air, air. Then Bogo sank, Jack beside him, both boys turning over to shoot down—down. They looked too wonderful to be human boys. The still, light blue water was shot through and through by moonlight and all things in it appeared beautiful. Below, the bottom came up to them like a floor of silver sand. Through silver vapour specked with pulsing dots of phosphorus they glided past a flowering rockery, where brilliant petals opened and shut, reached out and swayed, receded and dreamily reached out again. These flowers were live things that glowed like cups of liquid gold. There were star flowers seeking to outshine the stars far above; purple asters whose petals glowed in phosphorescent light; big rainbowed sea-carnations; snow-white sea-lilies. A giant eel flashed by a coral grotto, mysterious in plant and sea-animal life, with moving phosphorescent things.

Jack sped up to burst through a silver film and gasp in wonder to the moon. Bogo was smiling beside him.

"What do you think of it?" he murmured.

"Too beautiful for words," answered Jack when he got his breath. "I never dreamed of such a sea-floor at night—all lit by magic light."

"Neither is it as a rule. Generally the sea-floor is blacker than the pit. But among certain corals, in certain places at certain seasons, during the right weather, the underwater world is lit up as you have just seen. Full-moon time is a good time; the sea and moon appear far distant from one another, but really are very close. The moods of the moon are often the moods of the sea. But swim a little way with me, fill your lungs again and down we will go. You have seen little as yet."

Jack thought he had never seen Bogo's eyes so big and brown and bright. Bogo was smiling boyishly as he said: "When you breathe deep, glance up at the moon, try and inhale the light of the moon deep down into you. It sounds silly. But just try it."

Though puzzled, Jack obeyed.

Down they went again and the sea-floor came rising as grains of gold. A fish of quivering red with eyes of pearl flashed past. A tiny, green, pulsing bell glided towards Jack. He stared at the dull silver body of a fish with this lighted bell hung out on a drooping stem over its snout. That phosphorescent bell was what attracted smaller fish, and the big mouth engulfed them. Then Bogo glided ahead and Jack followed the silver soles of his feet. They glided through trellised shrubbery where long arms crept out to embrace them, soft feathery arms tinselled with sequins of coloured phosphoric bubbles. Strange eyes glared at them; huge eyes and little diamond eyes and glowing eyes that withdrew within stalk or flower.

Then something seemed to explode with a burst of wriggling water and the boys sped to the surface, enveloped in a cloud of brilliant bubbles.

"What was it?" gasped Jack.

"Leket le," said Bogo, "a big greeny-yellow thing shaped like the roof of a hut. In its top there is a little round hole that opens and shuts. That hole is mouth and eye. Around it are lots and lots of wriggly feelers. At full moon it fills up with air and phosphorus from the water. You must have kicked it, and then it blew out all those bubbles. It frightens fish that way when they come to eat it."

The fires on shore had died down; the warrior voices were silent. Jack dived again and saw other visions of loveliness. At last Bogo grew weary: "Come," he smiled, "we must sleep. We have a big day to-morrow."

9

THE FIGHT AT SEA

AT dawn fires were lit while spearmen won fresh fish from the lagoon. Breakfast was soon over, then several of the canoes were rowed out on to the lagoon. All hands dived and soon were popping up with the biggest oysters Jack had ever seen—as large as dinner-plates; really they were specimens of the pearl-shell oyster for which men throughout the ages have risked their lives. Jack swam down, saw the lithe forms gliding among the coral gardens, saw them shoot up to the surface clasping a big shell in each hand. He dived again and again but though his fingers fondled the bottom, though he searched amongst the grotesque shrubbery, he could not find a single oyster. He rose to the surface for the tenth time, panting in disgust.

"I'll show you," laughed Bogo. "Come on." They sped down through green twilight and glided in amongst a dim mound of seaweeds and sponges. Bogo turned and pointed. Jack glided up to him, stared at Bogo's hand which clutched a dull, greyish-white thing. Bogo wrenched hard and the big shell came *away.* Smaller shells grew upon it and a tiny coral fern and green weeds of the sea. No wonder Jack could not distinguish these camouflaged shells from the mass of corals and sea-ferns and sponges and animal-plant things amongst which they clung.

They sped to the surface and climbed aboard for a breather. The bottom of the canoe was now thickly covered with the big shells which the divers dropped while clinging to the canoe sides.

"The big shells are difficult to see, but you'll soon learn," said Bogo. "Keep a sharp look out for the 'eye'. It's not an eye really, it's the 'Up' of the shell. See."

He showed an open shell, gleaming with its mother-of-pearl. "The fish inside the shell eats when it is hungry," he explained, "and so must open just a wee bit. If your eyes are quick they see a glint like sun-light touching a bright stone. It is this shiny 'Up' that your eyes see. But if the fish hears you he closes his shell."

"How can it hear?"

"Easily. Haven't you heard sound when down below? Come on."

And down they dived. When below, Bogo clapped his hands and Jack heard the smack as if it was against his ear-drums. Then Bogo struck a stone and shell together and Jack heard a different sound. Then came utter silence again.

For several days they dived for the oysters while men ashore opened them and hung the meat on cords stretched between the masts, and out to the outriggers. Thus on the voyage the meat would be sun-drying. Dried, it is a delicacy. The beautiful shells were stacked in the canoes. The best of these would be cut and carved for ornaments, fish-hooks, gouges, knives, and other articles needing either beauty or strength. The remainder would be traded to New Guinea.

On the evening before sailing for fresh fields they yarned around the fires, throwing big oysters on the coals. These steamed in their own juice, popping open when cooked. The heat destroyed the shells, so the oysters whose shells were wanted were opened by knife. Jack was squatting there opening a huge oyster, the tough muscle of which resisted so strongly he had to use considerable force to open it. As his bone dagger cut the muscle he wrenched open the shell and a gleaming little object rolled into his hand. The warriors grunted and went on with their yarning and eating. Jack examined the beautiful object. He had never seen a real pearl, nor would he have believed that pearls came from oysters. This lovely gem which now glowed in his hand was worth a king's ransom, but he did not know that.

"What do you call it?" he asked Bogo.

"Myee," answered Bogo contemptuously. "They're pretty though, those wonder stones of the sea. Now and again you find an oyster that grows them. There are many in the shells that live on the great reefs of Tutu. The warriors there wear them through their noses as ornaments."

Jack thought he would keep this one as an ornament. He put it aside, but next morning in the bustle of departure it was forgotten.

They sailed to a light breeze, sunlight sparkling on dancing waves. To Jack it felt good to be alive. A small cloud appeared on the horizon; when he looked again it had grown surprisingly; soon it swelled into a dark cloud, twisting as it swiftly bore down on them.

"I think there's going to be a great storm," remarked Samsu gravely.

The canoemen gazed in alarm.

"Hadn't we better lower sail?" suggested Ramu anxiously.

"Not yet," replied Duppa gravely. "We'll wait and see."

The cloud was almost upon them when it swooped low to a mighty swish of wings. Wind fanned the men as feathers came floating down from the whirring cloud. For a long time it passed noisily by. There must have been a million mutton-birds in that great cloud.

As the canoes sped south-west keen-eyed spearmen in every bow watched for the rising of a turtle, ready to plunge the harpoon deep. At such times the rope would hiss out as the turtle dived for the depths, but quickly the weight of the canoe would exhaust it and it would rise to the surface. As the rope slackened, the canoe would shoot forward and when the turtle broke surface, men would leap overboard, throw the creature on its back and manhandle it aboard. Then the canoe would sail after the others.

Thus, the lucky canoe was left a little way behind, but the paddlers soon helped the sail to bridge the gap.

Hour by hour they sailed on, every now and then a canoe harpooning a luckless turtle that had arisen to bask on the sunlit surface. Bogo harpooned one that arose from under the very bows of the *War Chief.* Jack, now away behind in the *Sea Eagle,* echoed the shout of approval.

Towards sundown they approached a chain of low laying islands separated by reefs now bare in the low tide. These islets were uninhabited, but each look-out man. was alert for sign of smoke or life. From here, Marboo meant to cruise out to the sea-grass fields upon which the dugong feed.

And then the look-out man in the *Sea Eagle* harpooned a turtle. In a short time they slung him aboard and sailed after the canoes, now slightly ahead. Soon, though, a bowman harpooned another turtle, the crew cheering at their good fortune. They got this turtle aboard but had barely taken up the paddles when another rose just off the bows. Its alarmed head dived just as a harpoon pierced the shell.

"Good shot!" yelled Ramu.

By the time they tired him out and hauled him aboard the fleet was just gliding through a narrow passageway between two islands.

"All's clear," nodded Duppa. "They'll glide to anchorage in behind the larger island. I could eat a turtle on my own."

"Me too!" chorused the crew.

They took it leisurely now. And harpooned yet another turtle!

All hands shouted lustily. An omen! Four turtles one after the other was a sign that the good star Kek smiled upon every man in the canoe. Duppa rubbed his hands in pleasure as with cheery 'laughter, then increasing anxiety, they watched the rope spinning out. They must land this turtle or the promise of good luck would be broken.

This turtle took a long time to rise, but at last the rope slackened, the canoe shot ahead. Jack watched as anxiously as the others. As they peered over the bows they saw the turtle rising away below. The canoe flew ahead, six men leaped overboard as the turtle's gasping head broke surface, a monstrous turtle, a fighting loggerhead.

As hands snatched out for it, it snapped right and left with its vicious beak, struck convulsively with huge flippers, throwing itself around fair on the head of a man. Its great weight broke their grasp and down it dived. Shamefaced, they clambered aboard as the canoe gathered way. The loggerhead is a considerably larger and tougher customer to land than the green turtle, or the tortoise-shell.

Anxiously, silently, they followed the loggerhead. Again it rose to flounder as they threw themselves upon it. Its bulk rose from the water to dive with a mighty twist and splash.

Deep—deep—deeper it went as the rope spun out, then came a jerk and—silence. All stared at the rope - broken. They had lost Kek's turtle.

Duppa gazed around—then instantly roared "To paddles! To paddles!"

They sprang to it as a war-yell shrieked behind them—four canoes were almost upon them. Jack's hair rose on end. The canoe flew. The look-out man snatched up the Boo shell and out over the sea spread the loud, braying alarm.

Duppa gazed anxiously ahead towards the narrow passage between two coral walls. The steersman watched Duppa as behind them raced their howling pursuers. Two large canoes were straining to come up on the *Sea Eagle's* left, while two light canoes were racing to come up on the right. The larger canoes were coming one canoe length behind the others, now well within bow-shot. In moments now they would leap to the kill.

Duppa glanced back at the steersman, rolled his eyes, twisting his outstretched hand like the coding, darting neck of a snake, then nodded towards the left wall of the passageway, now very close. The steersman nodded, grinned from ear to ear, his big shoulders showing the strain of guiding the speeding canoe. "Be ready!" shouted Duppa. "We wheel and fight. Ease paddling the least little bit."

Immediately then the pursuers began to yell their gain. The *Sea Eagle* was just entering the passageway as the two larger canoes dashed up at her left. Duppa's hand shot out, the steersman lunged against the paddle, and the big canoe swerved straight for the wall of the reef.

"Down paddles! Weapons!" roared Duppa while a howl rose from the pursuing canoe as violently it swerved to avoid the *Sea Eagle* hissing past its bows. As Duppa's hand twisted right the steersman strained back against the paddle and the Sea *Eagle* swerved back directly across the bows of the dodging canoe. With a shriek they swerved too late, for the canoe behind crashed into them; her bow rose up and over them and seesawed down to nuzzle under the *Sea Eagle.* Violently the two light canoes swerved to avoid the wreckage.

In the pandemonium of shrieks and splintering wood Duppa's men leaped upon the wrecks, striking in a frenzy. Jack was amongst them, up to his knees in water, with, a sinking canoe underfoot. He went down under the struggling bodies and wreckage. He arose gasping in a wild melee with half the *Sea Eagle's* crew swimming, leaping, splashing aboard to snatch up bows and shoot. The enemy survivors dived, swimming under water, striving to reach shore before their lungs should burst. Jack splashed towards the *Sea Eagle* but a wounded savage grabbed him and convulsively dragged him down. Jack gouged his thumbs into the staring eyeballs and rose to the surface to plunge towards the *Sea Eagle,* now speeding shoreward.

The *War Chief* was coming with the flotilla at its heels, the two light canoes were paddling for their lives. A Boo brayed urgently and Jack saw something that made him shout and swim for dear life—a fleet of canoes racing behind Marboo's canoes. The flotilla had sailed into a trap that only an accident had sprung too soon. If Duppa's canoes had not been delayed by those four turtles, when the fleet had gone ashore, they would have found the enemy upon them and the passageway through the reef closed.

Duppa had glanced around to the Boo shell. Instantly he shouted orders and the *Sea Eagle* spun around to sea. Angry murmurs from the victorious crew, but one glance at the oncoming fleet, and they bent to the paddles—it meant their heads now.

Jack shouted despairingly, and Duppa frowned as he ordered the *Sea Eagle* pick up Jack. They hauled him aboard and turned to sea again as the *War Chief* came foaming up.

"Head the fleet," shouted Marboo, "straight for the sea—other canoes may be speeding out from the flanks ahead to cut us off."

Four grim heads hung from the tall bows of the *Sea Eagle,* no time for further trophies. Only five men of the *Sea Eagle* had been slightly wounded; the crashing of one canoe into the other had knocked the fight out of the sea-raiders. In compact form the flotilla sped on out into the darkening night. There was no sign of other enemy. The Boo brayed reassuringly and answer came from the anxious Marboo.

The pursuers were almost within arrow shot of the *War Chief,* guarding the rear. The enemy canoes, though smaller, far outnumbered those of Mer.

The *War Chief* was a battleship to a light cruiser compared to the largest of the enemy, and the leader of these urged his canoes on, not daring to tackle her with the two swiftest of his. But they could not bridge the gap between them and the formidable rearguard.

10

WHERE THE MUTTON-BIRDS BREED

From velvet night stars shone and then the moon turned the sea into rippling silver. Black velvet canoes raced across a silver sea. Not so beautiful the thoughts of the crews. One lot was racing to save their heads, the other to take them.

But the pursuers possessed neither the endurance nor the speed of the flotilla of Mer. Slowly but surely Marboo's vessels began to draw away, then faster until a shout went up. The pursuers were giving up the chase. With heaving chests and streaming brows, Marboo's men eased paddling, sails were lowered, laughter broke out, Bogo's shout to Jack came floating across from the *War Chief.*

"Did you get a head, Wak?"

"No. But I nearly lost one."

Thirstily they drank, then reached for half-cured oysters from the struts.

"I can still chew with my own head", grinned Awas.

"It's no use for anything else," laughed Kopam. "Not even ornamental."

"It looks nicer on my shoulders than decorating the masthead of a skull-hunter's canoe", retorted Awas as he munched.

The *War Chief* came creeping up to take the lead.

"I wonder where Marboo will sail to now," asked Baur.

"Any place where he thinks he can outwit danger and still carry on with the cruise," replied Saibo his mate. "But he won't push on until we've had a spell."

"I can do with a spell," sighed Tepem. "The old *Water Lily* is a log to paddle when you're racing for your head."

Marboo presently turned sou'-west, outwitting any chance of a further gathering of enemies. All that night the crews in watches, helped by the tides, steadily paddled towards the Great South Land which Jack would have called Australia. Had he known it, the *War Chiefs* bows were sailing to directly cut the course which the bosun's dinghy from the *Charles Eaton* had taken.

A wonderful historical course that, marking an undying chapter in the triumphs and tragedies of Australian sea history in our far north-east. The brave old Torres in his leaky tub gave his name to the Strait in 1606. Cook in the *Endeavour* rediscovered it for England in 1770. Marboo's canoes were now sailing to soon cut the course of an epic voyage that will never die, Captain Bligh's after the mutiny of the *Bounty* in 1789. Bligh also steered to meet the Australian coast, then voyage north, then west to Timor. It was Bligh who, in a later voyage in 1792, with the *Providence* and *Assistant,* again voyaged through Torres Strait and named Eroob Damley Island.

The canoes had already cut the course taken by the castaways from the frigate *Pandora,* wrecked on the Barrier Reef, not far from Mer, in 1791. It was Captain Edwards of the *Pandora* who named Mer Murray Island.

They had also cut the course of Bampton and Alt in the *Hormuzeer* and *Chesterfield* in 1793. When their whaleboat landed on Eroob the Erubians fiercely attacked them, killing five men. Of the survivors, only Ascott was not wounded; Shaw and Carter both were severely wounded. In the struggle they managed to scramble back into the boat, cut the anchor rope, and escape. Then, without provisions or compass there commenced for these three men another of those terrible yet wonderful voyages that have marked so many tragedies of, the Strait. They too made for Timor Laut and reached it, as did the bosun of the *Charles Eaton* so many years later.

Very soon Marboo's canoes were to cut the course of Matthew Flinders in the *Investigator* in 1802. Flinders was one of our greatest sea wanderers, and twice the canoes were to cut his course. After the wreck of the *Cato* and *Porpoise* on Wreck Reef in 1803 Flinders, with Captain Park and twelve men, rowed seven hundred miles in fourteen days to get help for the castaways left stranded on a sandbank, then sailed on the *Cumberland* on his next ill-fated voyage of discovery. He was again to pass through Torres Strait, only to be held prisoner by the French in Mauritius. He had left his wife as a bride in England, and it was to be nine years before he was to see her again.

Jack Ireland, when aboard the *Charles Eaton,* had listened to the crew discussing the voyages and fate of these and other great adventurers but never imagined that he was ever to live among savages, and by raft and canoe cross the "tracks" of all of them.

Next day was a dead calm. The canoemen paddled steadily until in late afternoon little clouds appeared, and swiftly spread as they rapidly came. The canoemen grunted and paddled a little stronger, with a glance at the sinking sun. Small, lowlying islands lay ahead, graceful pisonia-trees bright with yellow-green leaves stood above the sombre green of beach oak and wild fig. Jack, paddling with the *Sea Eagle's* crew, gazed at a mighty cloud fast approaching, so big and dark and far spreading as to dim the rays of the sun. That cloud was composed of armies of mutton-birds returning to their hungry families with food. In a shrieking medley of seabird language the clouds swept low to the sea and settled on the islands, the flapping of their wings, the greetings of comrades sweeping in noisy waves from island to island.

The canoes scraped up on to a tiny beach rough with dead coral, and gladly the men jumped overside and hurried to light fires and seize birds and eggs. Jack could barely hear the laughing shouts of Bogo above the nerve-racking cries of the birds. As they waddled to their nests they were greeted by thousands of hungry ones, while fresh battalions ceaselessly arriving, filled the air with wing-beats. The birds took no notice of the humans, so concerned were they with their own affairs.

Jack had hurried towards the trees loaded with nests but pulled up short when every step he took was on top of an indignant squawking mutton-bird. His feet broke through into burrows. In surprise he found that these birds nestled underground, dug out little tunnels so close together that his feet were continually breaking through into the home of some indignant family. Around his feet, clumsy, waddling, scolding birds were stepping into their burrows, self-important birds roughly abusing him for his big feet.

Mutton-birds are about the size of a small duck, dark brown in colour with a wedge-shaped tail and strong, red, hooked bill.

Jack gazed around to see the island a seething mass of birds, every square foot of the earth occupied; no matter where he placed a foot it was either on top of an angry mutton-bird or on top of a burrow. Stepping out cautiously he walked towards the low-branched trees, wondering why there were no birds in all those countless nests. He peered into a nest, then smiled in delight; the nest held five little white-caps all cuddled up together, a family of white-capped noddies in bed for the night. In every nest cuddled a similar cosy family.

The mutton-birds claimed all the ground, the noddies the trees. He counted two hundred nests in one tree. So vast in numbers were these two great families of birds that they could not have existed on the island had they not come to a friendly arrangement. Just before the mutton-birds came home each day, the noddies retired to bed. And that made room for the mutton-birds to alight and waddle to their own beds. Also, the noddies stayed in bed in the mornings until the mutton-birds flew away to their feeding-grounds. Thus did the birds keep out of each other's way.

Jack, hungrily diving on broiled mutton-bird, marvelled at the birds' common sense.

"There must be millions of them," he said. "How does each bird know how to go straight to his own nest?"

"How do you go straight to Duppa's house?" smiled Bogo.

"Well, how-does every bird know his own wife?"

"You'll learn that when you have one of your own," laughed Bogo. "If you make a mistake you'll know all about it."

"There must be great rows and squabbling when they come here each season and settle down."

"There is, but not so much confusion as you'd think. They go straight to the nest they used the year before. There are great rows of course if they find someone else in the old home; he is promptly thrown out. There is a lot of fighting too when they are choosing wives. The hen birds love to be fought over. It is only the young birds who seek wives; the old ones go back to their loves of the year before. We could hardly live on this island if we came here during the first month of the birds' arrival; then the island is like a great ant-bed with every ant in a raving hurry: searching for mates, love-making, cleaning out the old homes, building new ones. One would be smothered in flying leaves and sand; wouldn't be able to hear oneself talk night or day."

The crews ate ravenously, tired out but happy with this welcome change of food. The stars came twinkling, comparative quietness reigned, except that everywhere there seemed to be subterranean scoldings and bickerings.

Jack dug himself a sleeping-place and built a fire on either side. The weather, was warm but he knew that cold would come with the dawn. Although very hardy now, his bare skin still felt the changes in the. weather. A scooped-out bed in sand was easy to lie on. During windy nights he piled the sand beside him and thus slept sheltered from the wind.

A noisy squabbling awoke him. He sat up, shaking the sand from his hair. It was still dark, but in some mysterious way the island seemed to be moving. He stared all around. There lay the dark forms of his companions coiled in sleep; the dark shapes of the canoes. Glowing coals from fires burned low. But there was a shivery murmur in the air, and a distinct moving all over the island surface. Then a great squabbling.

"Noisy brutes!" grunted Bogo.

"What is happening?" asked Jack.

"It's only the mutton-birds getting ready to fly. Go to sleep."

But it was too interesting, and very soon too noisy for sleep: the marshalling of bird armies getting ready to fly with the dawn; the vanguards moving off in roars of beating wings.

11

A HAPPY CRUISE

The rim of a golden disk arose above the sea. A vast chorus greeted it. Jack stared at countless battalions of clumsy mutton-birds waddling importantly down to the shore, pushing and butting one another for footing space as they came in streams to swell the mobs massing along the beaches. From every burrow a mother bird scolded as she told her grumpy mate just what to do during the day, and ordered him to fly back well before sunset and not dawdle on the way.

In every burrow a dad or mum stayed behind to look after the baby, taking it in turn to stay home. Jack stood up and. looked towards the trees, the ground underneath seemed to be moving in dense, dark streams. He saw then that the birds had made many paths six feet wide under the trees, and down these they were crowding to the beach just as citizens crowd city footpaths at peak-hours. Now and again a bad-tempered bird would turn and fight, thus instantly holding up the traffic that would surge around the combatants with deafening scoldings. Occasionally, too, a gentleman bird would choose this time to be courteous to a lady friend, and they would cluck and purr together, taking no notice of the indignation aroused. Jack laughed at the leave-taking at the mouth of every burrow, the two birds noisily talking, to at last kiss with a cluck and purr, when the breadwinner waddled away to join the crowds waddling to the beach.

Running down the slopes the birds took off in little mobs that quickly swelled to great clouds, noisy as a wind-storm.

As the last cloud whirred up into the fast brightening sky, the island grew quiet—for a moment. Then, from hundreds of nests upon thousands of trees little white-caps peeped up, and the cheery little noddies appeared with their fluffy families around them. Now the island belonged to the terns for the day. Every tree seemed massed with white flowers which were the heads of the noddies.

"Wonderful!" said Jack. "Like a great city used by two different nations. A city teeming with inhabitants, yet so well organized that both nations live happily in it without ever getting in one another's way."

For the next few days all hands were busy preparing and smoke-drying mutton-birds sufficiently to preserve them until they returned to Mer. As Jack worked he turned to Bogo and said:

"We are like the mutton-birds. We seek fish or turtle by day, while the women stay at home and look after the family. The mutton-birds leave home by day also to gather food, although husband and wife take it in turn to stay home. They return at sundown with food for the family. And here are we, far from home, seeking food to take back to the families."

"Yes," smiled Bogo, "we are all families, men and birds and animals and fishes. And we've all got to work and hunt for food."

When the flotilla sailed they cruised a few days along the coast of the Great South Land, parallel to the track that the ill-fated Kennedy took when years later he explored the east coast of Cape York Peninsula. Marboo then steered east, lazily sailing out towards the Great Barrier Reef. For he wished to load up with rare shells and oil and fish skins from great and queer fishes, not found around the reefs of Mer.

"Wonders of the sea live deep down among the mystery caverns of the Father of Reefs," explained Duppa to Jack. "Fish of great size seldom seen anywhere else, giant turtle and shellfish, big eels and sea-snakes. The livers of some among these contain oils good to eat and for medicines; the skins of some are thick and strong; others contain juices that dye our ceremonial feathers beautiful colours. There, too, we find most of the shells with which we trade to New Guinea for arrows and feathers and canoes, and many other things. The New Guinea people want these shells because their own waters hold none like them."

"Are the big fish dangerous?" asked Jack.

"Not at all. There are monsters larger than this canoe but harmless if left alone. Others have great mouths armed with rows of teeth, mouths like, a tunnel, down which a man could go. These lurk in the coral caverns deep below. One snap, and a man's arm or leg is gone."

"Do you ever lose any men out there?"

"Sometimes. Last season Kaba dived down. He was bitten clean in halves."

Jack resolved to be very careful.

"We seldom lose a man," explained Duppa, "because experience has taught us that to take an unnecessary chance is foolish."

Next day they were fishing with spears along a coral reef exposed by the low tide. It stretched away for several miles, its waters lovely with gardens, through which darted clouds of rosy coral fish with silver eyes and tails and fins. Jack and Bogo went wading along the reef with their spears half poised, eyes watchful. Jack picked up a lovely shell, but quickly dropped it as a scarlet crab hopped out and slithered to the water.

"He hasn't a shell of his own," laughed Bogo, "so he squeezes into an empty shell and carries it about as his home. If he didn't, the others would eat him."

"But he must grow inside that shell", said Jack.

"Of course. When he grows too big for the shell he searches around, finds a larger one that will fit him, makes sure no enemy is watching, then hurriedly changes his home."

"There appear to be plenty of crabs about, of all sorts and sizes."

"There are more crabs than there were birds on that mutton-bird island. Only you've got to use your eyes to see them. You're nearly standing on one now, it's a wonder he doesn't nip your toe."

Jack stared down at his feet among corals and plant-life, but saw no sign of a crab. Bogo touched a pretty little plant with the haft of his spear and laughed as it scuttled away.

"That crab covers himself with weeds so that enemies can't see him," explained Bogo; "he carries the weeds with him wherever he goes. There's another sort of crab who is a real gardener. He cuts tiny slips and roots of weeds with his nippers, plants them in the joints of his shell, and anchors them there with little hairs that curl around the leaves like tendrils curl around vines. Then those tiny bits of sea leaves sprout and grow."

"But," objected Jack, "the plants would grow so large that the crab couldn't carry the garden around with him."

"He keeps the plants trimmed, just as we trim our gardens on Mer. Even so, the plants grow so fast that a lazy crab couldn't move if the water and tide didn't buoy up the garden on his back. When the garden grows all over a lazy fellow he just waits about and gorges (for more food flows around him than he can eat) till the time comes for him to cast off the old shell for a new one. Then he nips off tiny cuttings from the old garden and starts another on his new shell."

"Jolly clever," laughed Jack. "Surely the crab must think?"

"He certainly appears to think. I could talk for hours about the many cunning things crabs do. There are other little crabs that not only carry a garden on their backs to hide them from enemies and at the same time collect unsuspecting food, but they really become part of the garden. When such a crab travels or is forced from his hunting-grounds he often finds himself where the coral gardens grow different coloured plants to those he grows on his back. This difference might easily betray him to some sharp-eyed enemy. So he nips the garden off his back and plants a new one, using the coloured plants that grow in his new home. Thus no hungry enemy is likely to suspect him of being a crab."

As they waded along, Bogo pointed to a clear coral pool with a bottom of clean white sand: "What do you see on the very bottom of that pool?" he asked.

"White sand," said Jack, "and a couple of spiny sea-urchins, a black *bêche-de-mer* and a red prickly one... And those tiny fish with the 'eye' painted on the centre of the body... Oh, and there's a baby turtle just poking out from the coral near that sea star."

"Do you see a crab right in the very centre of the white sand, between the sea-urchin and star?"

"No."

Bogo prodded the pool with his spear-haft and a white crab scuttled across the bottom, to stop abruptly near a big, flat, greenish animal-plant. Swiftly it changed colour to grey, then light green, then a dark green like the plant. Jack had now to look closely to see the crab!

"That's how these crabs hide from their enemies," explained Bogo. "They change colour when they travel over different coloured sands or corals or plants. It is not so easy to see or follow them."

"It might save us if we could change the colour of our skins like that," said Jack, "if ever we are chased by the skull-hunters."

"We'd have to change colour very quickly. You, yourself, can change colour."

"How?"

"You *have* changed. When the Aureed skull-hunters caught you they said you were the colour of the Lamars, white as that white sand you could not see the white crab upon. Now, you are nearly as brown as I am.

12

THE SHARK

"Look!" exclaimed Bogo pointing into deep water. "Did you see him?"

"What?" peered Jack.

"A crayfish!" and Bogo smiled in delight. "They're lovely to eat, sweet meat that melts in your mouth. Quick, we'll go back for the small canoe; we can dive better from her than from the reef. Don't tell the men; we'll surprise them."

As they paddled the canoe along beside the reef Bogo explained:

"Sea crayfish are much like lobsters, only smaller and prettily coloured. They're not armed with big nippers; but they grow rows of spikes along their backs, and if you grasp the cray the wrong way those spikes will rip the skin off your hands. When the crayfish swims he kicks sharply behind and under with his tail, and shoots backward. Which is surprising, if you grip him the wrong way. Watch me when we dive; I'll show you. But we'll spear all we can; it's quicker. Here we are now, right above their village. The crayfish, like mutton-birds, often live together."

Bogo put his face to the water, and stared down.

In that bright sunlit sea, during the sou'-east season, the water is the clearest sea-water in the world. The boys could see the mysterious coral gardens far below; see fish swimming about, and large bailer shellfish crawling along the bottom. But the shellfish and a vivid blue starfish also were only visible where clean sand showed amid the riot of plant-life.

"Ah! I saw one shoot across that cliff away down there; he's gone to the crayfish home", laughed Bogo. "Come on, we'll go down and I'll point them out. You'll see their eyes twinkling like tiny water stars."

The boys slipped overboard and held on while they filled their lungs, then sank, to turn over and glide straight down among staghorn corals, and luxuriant under-sea plants upon which green snails fed. Bogo glided over a coral rockery, Jack beside him. Suddenly, Bogo pointed. Jack saw nothing but a garden of fantastic shapes with coloured shrubs and sea-flowers of gold and white, of red and blue; and in among it all a lively swarm of little coloured fish. Bogo thrust swiftly and the spear-head vanished down a coral cranny. The movement of the spear showed it had impaled something. Bogo wrenched up the spear and on its point was a big crayfish kicking violently. As they turned to swim up, a pointed thing shot past with a sound like a clap of hands, to vanish backward into a coral crack. It was a startled crayfish making for home.

When they reached surface Jack curiously examined the first sea crayfish he had ever seen.

"See these two long 'stalks' growing out from its head?" said Bogo. "Well, here are its eyes on the end of them, like tiny, shiny water pebbles. By twisting these stalks around it can see in all directions. Those eyes shine down below, just like -the. bright lip of the big oyster. You watch for the glint from the lip of the oyster, and you watch for the glint from the eye of the crayfish. See these long threads growing out near its 'mouth'? Well, if you twist them around your fingers like this you can pull him from the deepest crack. He daren't kick; it hurts too much. But unless you grip these 'whiskers' in just the right way, he kicks and they break. You must be very cunning and quick before you can catch hold of them at all. But you'll learn. Still, it's much easier to spear them. But be careful they don't kick off the prongs; they're strong and quick. Come on, there are a lot of them down there."

Down they went, and now Jack knew what to look for. He glided over waving tendrils and seamaid's hair, not knowing how big and staring his own eyes were as he swam looking for other eyes— and saw them. Like tiny diamonds flashing among the sea-grasses, now here now there, as the inquisitive owners stared at the men things. Jack thrust at two wee diamond eyes, but they popped back amongst the corals. He thrust at several others but these vanished too. He heard a sharp clap, then clap again as two crays shot backward past him.

"Missed!" he thought and swam, up for air. Far above he saw the soles of Bogo's feet just breaking surface and knew that Bogo would have another crayfish. He determined to get one the very next dive.

And he did. But was fortunate, for there is a knack in finding, spearing, and securing a sea crayfish; generally experience is necessary. Jack had to hunt for his very living, and this necessity compelled him to learn by every experience.

The boys enjoyed this game of hide-and-seek and skill. Bogo was happy at the thought of the men's pleasure when they saw this luxury added to the larder. They arose for a breather. Presently Jack said:

"I'm going down again."

"You're eager," smiled Bogo, "but it's the quickest way to learn. Better rest your lungs a few minutes longer, though; because you take in just a little less air, and a little less each time you dive, unless you rest long enough in between every few dives."

"I'm all right," said Jack, and loosening his grip of the canoe, sped rapidly down.

As he reached bottom a shadow sped above him— and his blood ran cold. He whipped around and the shadow with terrible, cold eyes came at him. He snatched at the bottom and lay pressed in among the weeds as the shark sped by. Bogo had told him that if a tiger shark ever appeared between him and the surface to grasp the bottom and hold hard. The shark might even try to turn him over with its nose, for if he was pressed flat in amongst the coral it could not get a bite at him. The shark might circle, then speed swiftly back. Circle the second time—and speed swiftly back. Circle the third time out of sight —and that was the chance for the diver to put all his last desperate strength into reaching the surface. Otherwise, he never would.

Jack clung frantically as a raspy, clammy snout came poking through the weeds, two cold, evil eyes above him. He felt a vicious thud as the snout tried to turn him over. But he was wedged too tightly in between the corals.

The shark vanished. Jack tried to quieten his heart, to keep calm and save every bubble of air within him. The steel-grey shadow glided just over him, vanished again. Jack waited. Would it never come! He felt his lungs would burst; he could never hold on if it did not come soon. It came; hovered there; then vanished.

Jack shot up through green twilight. He knew he was done. In an agony of fear he kicked out, saw the bottom of the canoe, saw Bogo's legs dangling up there where was God's own blessed air and sky.

The tiger of the sea was coming. Jack struck out; saw Bogo's face pressed to the water surface, then Bogo come shooting straight down with the long bone dagger in his hand; saw the shark's eyes; saw a flash of belly as the dagger sunk deep; felt the swirl as he struggled up to grasp the canoe. With a terrible gasp he snatched an outrigger and weakly clung until Bogo's arm was around him.

"Quick", said Bogo, "climb aboard before others come—the scent of blood will bring them. Ah! the thought makes you move. There now! We're right. Aboard the canoe we can laugh at the sharks. But that big fellow has sped to the depths with my best dagger", he added ruefully. Jack lay panting, staring up at the sky. He clutched Bogo's arm.

"I—I'll never forget you, Bogo", he gasped.

Bogo laughed awkwardly. "It was nothing," he muttered. " You would have done the same for me. I loved doing it, I would love to do something like that every day, I want to be a warrior—a great warrior. Besides—it was my fault."

"Your fault!" gasped Jack.

"Yes," answered Bogo seriously. "I should have told you, Jack. I forgot you would not remember, you who have been a Lamar. Sharks love crayfish, just as men do. And sharks seek crayfish eagerly, just as men do. When a shark hears a crayfish clap his tail he comes quickly. If the tide towards him is favourable, you could hardly believe from how far away a shark can hear a crayfish. The crayfish can swim without making that sound; he only makes it violently when he plunges to escape an enemy. There were many crayfish down below; we hunted them, and they struggled to kick away from the spears and us. That cruising tiger heard the kicks—and came. I should have warned you of the danger."

"It would have made no difference," said Jack weakly.

"Yes it would. You would have been prepared for what might happen. Both of us would have been more careful."

"What made you gaze down?" asked Jack.

"I suddenly thought of sharks; thought you had been down a long time. I saw you—saw the shark."

"I'll never forget," said Jack.

"It was nothing," laughed Bogo and jumped up. "Come. To the paddles. The tide has turned. See, along the reef the men are gathering together and lighting the fires. They are hungry."

They pulled back along the reef and laughed to shouts of good-natured banter.

"Here come the idlers," shouted Ikari, "to eat our fish."

"You don't know what real fish are!" shouted Bogo. "Keep your fish—we dine on meat."

"So the young warriors have got no fish," laughed Nara. "They come to dine on our mutton-birds."

Bogo held up a crayfish. A shout of delight greeted them as they jumped out on to the reef.

"Where did you get them?" asked Waroo. He had been fishing far along the reef.

Bogo pointed back along the reefs.

"We will all go," said Waroo eagerly, "and get crayfish for all."

Bogo shook his head. "A shark came!" he said soberly.

Then Jack stepped forward to Marboo the Chief. And in front of them all he told the story; told Marboo his son had proved that the blood of warriors ran in his veins; told them how he owed his life to Bogo.

Marboo listened with expressionless face. Jack was certain he was pleased, until suddenly he turned on his son, his face distorted with passion. Fiercely he threatened him. Jack angrily protested, but Marboo turned on him, and Jack saw in those furious eyes the look he had seen on the face of Cut-cut of Aureed. Marboo controlled himself with a violent effort and turning, strode away along the reef. The men quickly turned to the cooking-fires.

Jack laid his hand on Bogo's shoulder. Bogo smiled, shook off the comforting hand and went and sat down by' himself. Jack was bewildered. Instead of Bogo receiving praise for a very gallant deed here he was shamed by his own father before all the men. He saw Duppa's troubled eyes upon him. He walked up to the old warrior and Duppa laid his hand upon his shoulder.

"I send praise to the Great Ones through the Zogo that you are spared, my son," he murmured.

Jack was touched, and very troubled.

"My heart is sore, father-mer," he said. "Tell me, why did Marboo the Chief thunder against his brave son so."

"Bogo did wrong," answered Duppa gravely. "He should have told us that he had found crayfish. Then we would have all dived together and got many crayfish-before sharks came. If they had come there would have been so many of us that none but the hungriest shark would have dared attack. As it is, we have got but few crayfish and now dare not risk the sharks. Mer nearly lost a man, and Duppa—a son."

Presently, Jack took his cooked fish to Bogo and tried hard to share with him. But Bogo would not eat. Jack was fast learning that not only had he always to act, he was also always expected to think. Sitting there silently beside Bogo, he puzzled it all out.

He, and all these people, had to fight and work to exist. Had Bogo told all hands about that crayfish colony, then every man would be eating crayfish this night, with but little risk of a man having been lost to a shark. Bogo, son of a chief, was some day to be a chief. But he would never be a successful chief if he did not think of all his people first.

Jack saw that Marboo in punishing his son was really teaching him a lesson that would help fit him for chieftainship.

13

THE WHALES

Several days later the canoes were sailing lazily east, no sign of land. A dreamy sea, brilliant sunlight, only a puffy breeze. Snatches of song rose from the canoes, jokes were shouted from canoe to canoe. Jack, standing away out on an outrigger, was staring far ahead to what appeared like a wispy line of smoke stretching far as the eye could see. Distantly came a murmuring like thunder.

"The Father of Reefs," smiled Duppa, "sings contentedly to-day."

"That smoke then is spray from rollers breaking on the great reef?"

Duppa nodded.

"Another sea comes in from far out there," he explained. "A sea that rises we know not where. That sea comes rolling in towards the Great South Land until out there it crashes against the Father of Reefs. Deep water there, for the coral wall goes down deeper than the steepest cliffs of Mer. Many days' sail south far past where your eyes can no longer see the 'smoke', the Father still runs his great wall. That wall protects all the islands, and the coast of the Great South Land from the wrath of the Big Sea."

Jack knew this only vaguely, although in the *Charles Eaton* he had sailed up here into the Coral Sea parallel with the Great Barrier Reef, with the hazy Queensland coast to the west. But though from the ship's deck he had seen foam breaking on many a reef, he had never imagined such a mighty wall as this. How could he? The Great Barrier Reef runs for twelve hundred miles, from just south of New Guinea to a little north of Bundaberg, Queensland.

"We really are sailing on one sea then," he said, "and gazing on another out past those columns of spray."

"Yes. Out past the Father of Reefs is the Father of Seas. Our sea, the sea inside the reef and among all the islands right to New Guinea is a baby sea to the Big Sea. Our sea is very shallow, compared to the Big Sea. The colour of our sea is a light green, as shallow water generally is. The colour of the Big Sea is a deep blue. We can dive nearly anywhere in our sea and reach bottom, but a man could dive in the Big Sea and go down and down and find only the black world of the under-sea."

"From Mer," said Jack, "we have sailed many days, and every day have seen reefs. What then are all these reefs?"

"Children of the Father," smiled Duppa, "like children of the tribe.

Mer has many people, many children. Our allies are Eroob with the people of Eroob, and Ugar with the people of Ugar. And of us, Mer is the greatest and strongest, the father of our people. And among all the island nations the alliance of Mer and Eroob and Ugar is the greatest, stronger than the alliance of the western islands, and the central islands, and the tiny people in between. We are stronger even" he added proudly, "than the great sea warriors of Tutu. But—we are all people, all islands. The Great South Land and Great New Guinea are the mothers of islands. The Father of Reefs is the father of reefs. Men are men, but some nations are greater than others. And the Father of Reefs is the greatest of all reefs."

A hail came from the *War Chief.* Bogo dived from the stem, and arose lazing in the water, awaiting the oncoming *Sea Eagle.* Laughingly he climbed aboard. Bogo was forgiven. For the future he would think for all before he acted, as behoves the son of a chief.

"A great sight!" he said, waving towards the wall of spray. Lazy rollers from the long swell of the Pacific were tumbling upon the reef to break in murmuring thunder, rapidly growing louder as the falling tide exposed the reef. The green of the sea was broken by a vast belt of dazzling foam. Plainly now for miles columns of spray and vapour shot up and filled the air with a ceaseless, thunderous roar. The seaward side of the mighty wall was a tumult of pounding seas, but on their landward side peaceful green water was sparkling under sunlight.

To a shout of alarm a black mass arose beside the *Sea Eagle,* and breaking water with a great splash, rose high and gazed at them from little eyes. A subterranean cough, a rumbling gurgle, and they were splattered with warm air and water. The whale lay there rumbling and' spluttering, regarding them curiously. Jack stared fascinated at that mountain of shiny black, longer than the canoe and much larger. In amazement he saw sucker-fish clinging to it while clammy sea-grass and shellfish grew on its hide. The steersman bent to his oar, striving to steer gradually away from the whale. An outrigger pole scraped its side, and it twitched with pleasure to the tickling. It rolled a bit, exposing its underside, as if inviting this strange friend to scrape off those itchy shellfish. The crew held their breaths. One lazy swipe of that mighty tail and the *Sea Eagle* would be crushed to splinters.

To a noisy splash, another carcass arose between two canoes. Then came splash after splash, gurglings and blowings, spoutings of air mixed with spurts of water. A school of whales had risen among, all around, ahead and astern, of the canoes. They now sailed in the centre of the school which was travelling south, parallel with the reef. Marboo headed the *War Chief* south, for to keep sailing across the shoal would have meant collision and disaster. They must sail with the school, hoping they would gradually swim by.

But they did not. Their pace was exactly that of the canoes. Jack watched fascinated as the lazy monsters swam effortlessly, obviously filled with an overwhelming curiosity about the canoes. Beside each canoe there swam a slate-grey bulk. The one beside the *War Chief* was gigantic, its mountainous back rose high as the fighting platform of the war canoe.

"It is fitting," said Duppa grimly, "that the chief of the whales should swim beside the chief of the canoes."

"But it should be in the lead," said Bogo, staring anxiously.

"Not always. Your father's canoe was in the lead until the savages ambushed us away back there. Then he directed the canoes from the centre, then fell back to the rear when danger threatened from there."

"I'm going to swim for it," said Bogo. "I should never have left my father's canoe."

"You had his permission," answered Duppa. "All is well. Do not leave the *Sea Eagle.* To dive overboard might disturb the whales and thus you might bring disaster upon us all."

As the canoes sailed on and nothing happened, Jack stood on the tall stern, gazing around with thrilled interest. Far as thc eye could see ahead were the big dark bodies of whales lazily leading the cruise. He gazed astern, and as far as he could see were whales. Across to the 'west whales were visible another mile. And they stretched east right to the edge of the reef. He gazed down at the big fellow waddling along beside them, and recognized the sucking-fishes clinging to its sides. It was with similar fish that the Aureed men used to locate turtles, if none were visible. They would tie a long cord to the fish's tail and throw it overboard above a feeding-ground. It would swim down below as the canoe drifted, and if it located a turtle, would attach itself to it by suction. Thus by the pull on the cord the savages would locate their turtle. We call this quaint fish the remora.

The men except two in each canoe stood to the paddles, ready for any manoeuvre should danger threaten. Two men in each canoe stood with long bamboo poles, now and then gently prodding any whale that came dangerously close. And now Iraki prodded the big fellow Jack was gazing at:

"Just keep off a bit, old good-for-nothing," said Iraki coaxingly. "If only you would come ashore we'd feast on your meat for many a day. But you are master here, so don't make us food for the sharks. Now keep off—do."

And he prodded the big nose stoutly but not too hard, scolding it as a father would a child. Raroo stood by the stern and similarly prodded when the great tail drew too near. The whale would sheer off, but seeming to like it, gradually he would draw very close again.

"You want us to prod those barnacles," said Iraki soothingly; "but we won't, because then you'd never leave us. And above all, we want to see the last of you. If you wish to be rid of those bitey barnacles, why don't you dive and scrape them off against the Father of Reefs?"

Jack laughed.

"I wish I was aboard my father's canoe," smiled Bogo mournfully. "Then I could laugh too. It would be great fun."

"Anyway, you are not in the wrong this time," consoled Jack, "so laugh while we may. What would you do if the whale smashed the canoe?"

"Dive deep—towards the great reef. When I came up I'd look around to see if I could help anyone. If not, I'd swim for a canoe. If I couldn't reach one I'd swim on to the reef."

"Of course," said Jack. "I did not think of that. The canoes would sooner or later pick us up off the reef."

"Yes—if they could do so in time."

"In time?"

"Yes. When the tide comes in, it will cover the reef."

Bogo laughed at Jack's face.

"Does this happen always on big fishing-trips?" asked Jack of Duppa.

"Not often. We always see whales, but the sea is wide; it is unusual for canoes to be caught right among a big school. Often though a whale, or two or three whales will follow a canoe for a day, sometimes through the night too. At such times we make a great noise and slap the water with paddles. It scares them away as a rule.

"But we daren't alarm this school; there are too many of them, and too many canoes. If they become alarmed some would surely smash a canoe."

"They don't look savage."

"They're not; they are clumsy and curious. It is their great weight and stupidity that does the damage when alarmed—unless one is hurt, then he will turn ' on a canoe in fury."

"There is no real danger then?"

"There is always a little danger. If it enters the stupid head of this big fellow here that now is a great chance to rub those barnacles off his back, then he'll simply do it. He'll turn and dive under the *Sea Eagle* and come up under the bottom. He'll use the *Sea Eagle* as a scraper, and we'll all go tumbling into the sea."

"I hope he doesn't think the thought," said Jack. "If he does," answered Duppa grimly, "dive deep. For when the canoe and all of us begin tumbling all over him he'll become alarmed and lift that tail of his higher than the canoe. And when that tail comes down there'll be no canoe left, and no men— if the tail hits them."

"Has that happened before?"

"Seldom. But then, all things happen through the courses of the years at sea."

All day long the canoes were escorted by the whales; there was no escape. When Marboo slowed down the canoes and attempted to drift behind, the whales slowed down too; it almost seemed that some mysterious signal passed from one to the other far away ahead, far away to the rear. Whales and canoes lazily glided on to the thunder of the rollers on the reef. Jack gazed towards the roar of sound, the line of spray dashing high into the air: "What mighty strength must be in that reef that it withstands the waves day and night, year by year."

"During storms," said Duppa, "no man can shout against the thunder that rises there."

"No man could live."

"Oh, yes, a fleet can live. Terror and destruction can rage across on the Big Sea side of the reef, while a fleet shelters safely on this side—unless the wind changes."

"Then it would blow the fleet on to the reef?"

"Yes."

"And that would mean?"

"Boigu—Isle of the Blessed," said Duppa grimly.

Afternoon came and went, and still they sailed with the whales. Night came, the stars shone out, the great reef quietened as the tide came swirling in and cushioned the coral against the break of the waves. But ghostly spray still shot up, and all things appeared beautiful.

With the night gradually came a deep calm, through which came the dull rumble from the reef; heavy murmurings, deep sighs and grunts from the whales.

Jack was startled now and again as the big fellow, again beside the *Sea Eagle,* rumbled deep down and coughed air and spray.

Then suddenly, in the middle of the night, the whales gathered speed as if by magic. Jack watched the big fellow forge ahead almost regretfully; he had come to almost like him.

The canoes were almost stationary. For an hour Jack watched big black shapes coming up out of the night to glide swiftly by in a bath of coloured phosphorus. Then a sigh of relief, shouts of thankfulness from the canoes. Out flashed the paddles as each canoe turned towards the great reef. They anchored to the coral edge and immediately sprawled down in the canoes to sleep.

The boys see the apparition that scared their native friends.

14

DEATH FROM THE DEPTHS

At dawn the canoes sailed north, back the way they had come yesterday. A beautiful, dawn, though not a breath of wind. Rhythmically the paddles dipped to the deep-chested song of the rowers. Marboo leading with the *War Chief,* gazed earnestly at the sky and the silent sea. Everything was as it should be. The wild nor'-west season at earliest was not due at least until the passing of the moon. But Marboo felt slightly uneasy.

He frowned. But for those whales they would have spent yesterday and last night on the dugongs' feeding-grounds. He was now steering straight, back along the reef, towards Mer. By sunset they would reach the shelling-grounds. They would load up, then voyage to dugong grounds still farther north— not so good as along the great reef, but if weather threatened they would be within easy sail of Mer.

Easy in his mind, Marboo joined his voice to the rise and fall of the sweet canoe song of the Torres Strait islanders. Jack sang too; even in customs and of the very lives of the people. He was one of them.

By midday the sea shone like liquid glass; there was only a gentle murmuring away across the great reef for an unusual calm was upon the Pacific.

Suddenly the bow man shouted, the steerman swerved and the canoe grazed by a monster rising under the very bows. Jack stared as a leathery head large as a football broke surface; its shell followed, broader than a capsized dinghy. A wheeze like a leaky steam engine attracted every ear. Deep whistlings, hoarse gasps came from the giant beak. Solemn eyes like big marbles stared up at the men. All hands ceased paddling, Jack gazed at this monstrous turtle that might have arisen straight up out of primal ages.

Running the length of its arched back was a ridge of horny bone that Jack instantly likened to the keel of a dinghy. Its greeny-yellow carapace appeared more like plates of inch-thick bone than turtle-shell. These plates slowly moved as it sucked in air. They were joined underneath with a thick, pliable skin tougher far than the webbed skin that joins a duck's toes. As slowly it inhaled air, so the plates gently moved and occasionally would spread quite apart. Then every plate would come together, and the whole vast shell be as immovable as a dome of steel. Each flipper appeared the size of an ordinary turtle. The canoes crowded around, the men gazing at this monster, the like of which even they had seldom seen. "What is it?" asked Jack in awe.

"The Father of Turtles," laughed Duppa. "The Father of Reefs, as you will learn when you have voyaged here as often as I have, is the home that feeds the great things of the sea. You must make many trips here; dive down deep before you see them all. And when you are an old man, there will still be great children of the Father of Reefs that you will not have seen."

"Is he of any use?" asked Jack.

"If we could kill or capture him we would surely make use of him. But no harpoon yet made by us can pierce that bone, nor could any rope hold him. Turtles like him live at great depth and seldom arise. Or if they do, it must be at night-time. Occasionally, we have seen one out from the shores of Mer."

The *War Chief* began to draw ahead, Marboo was impatient to be off. Slowly canoe after canoe followed. Jack was sorry to feel the *Sea Eagle* drawing away; he could have watched that quiet monster a long time. The last canoe to leave was captained by a young warrior holding his first command, and the young men aboard were keen to sport with the turtle while a few moments yet remained. Young Barza stepped from an outrigger and stood upon the great back, laughter arose as Tobun followed him. Barza stood on his head, Tobun jumped up and down on the turtle's back, but the creature merely turned its neck and noisily hissed. Two other young fellows leaped down upon it, and all four commenced a war-dance. But the creature took no more notice of them than if they had been rabbits.

Bogo was watching from the *War Chief,* Jack looking on from the *Sea Eagle.* Young Barza squatted down on the turtle, and digging his fingers in between the plates, began to ride it with heels and back. Tobun squatted behind him and got a grip too.

"Leave go!" roared Duppa. "Take your fingers out—"

The beast began to submerge. Fear made ashen the young men's faces—their fingers were jammed between the fast-closed plates of shell. They struggled desperately. Their mates snatched at their legs as they vanished. Others dived overboard with any weapon they could snatch.

One by one the swimmers came to the surface. Last came gasping men supporting the two who had clung to the legs of Barza and Tobun. Their eyes told awful things: '

"We hung on," gasped one at last, "until we could hold—no longer. They—have gone!"

In fury Marboo turned on the captain of the canoe. Useless for him to plead "he did not know!"

"You know nothing!" roared Marboo. "What was there for you to know but to follow me! I moved off, you stayed behind!"

Jack felt sorry for the captain as he had for Bogo. But again Marboo was right. Every canoe should have followed when the chief led off. His the responsibility, his to know things for the good of all.

They cruised in circles for two silent hours but neither body came up.

Then the *War Chief* moved off; silently the others followed.

"You knew it might happen," said Jack to Duppa, "when you shouted warning. Have you seen it happen before?"

"Once, when I was young as you, just after my first initiation, and on my first long cruise, as this cruise is yours. And it happened just the same way. I had forgotten, until young Barza dug his fingers down below the plates. I should have shouted before, but how was I to foretell that a thing of forty years ago was to happen again today? It was written in the Courses of the Stars."

They paddled on all that day and far into the night. Next day with their canoes drawn up along the edge of the great reef, the canoemen were diving busily, quickly. Gone was the cheery joke, the snatches of song, the laughter. These were men anxious-to load and be safe home again. The loss of Barza and Tobun was a bad omen.

"We had a wonderful cruise," muttered Ikari, "a successful fight against the skull-hunters, the canoes part loaded with smoked fish, turtle, sun-dried oysters, and smoked mutton-birds. We would have loaded with trade shell, then dugong oil and meat. But now our cruise is bitter. We must return singing the Death Wail."

Jack worked as hard as the others. They sought shellfish now that were of value in trade with New Guinea. Jack had once believed that all shells could simply be picked up on a sea beach. He knew now that "live" shells had shellfish inside them, which lived only on suitable feeding-ground, generally in particular seasons and at varying depths in the sea.

Jack dived down past a cliff draped in clinging vines and flowers, among which swam golden pansies dotted with crimson. Eyes of fish glistened diamond bright as they sped past. Down he glided and a cavern opened out, curtained with sea-fronds. As he glided past a big groper swam into the cavern and, turning, stared at him from monstrous eyes of baleful green. Down, down he went, gazing anxiously amongst coral columns, all rose coloured in the green twilight.

He thought he saw a shellfish hidden amongst sea-grass and reached in as a huge claw clashed out at him. Had that giant crab gripped his fingers, they would have been shorn off. But now he saw several large shellfish, though not the kind he sought. Yes, climbing up a coral-head a bright shell large as a helmet, with the owner's long, thick neck stretching out as it reached for a grip higher up. The bright blue neck and head were of thick flesh, while firm, blue flesh gripped the coral-head from underneath the shell. Out from the head stood two fleshy horns from which queer, bulging eyes gazed this way and that.

Jack seized it; his air was almost exhausted. In a flash the head disappeared as it gripped with the strength of a vice. But Jack knew the secret; he jerked sharply upward and the flesh lost its grip as if it had slid from a greasy pole. With the heavy shellfish held tight, he shot upward through green twilight that swiftly grew brighter until he could see the canoes, then the sky resting above. He popped up, gasping for air.

All that morning they worked steadily, and the fishing was very good. Conch, cone, and other valuable shellfish were dining among the luxurious coral gardens below.

Early that afternoon Jack was swimming down, down past domes and caves and pinnacles, where coloured things winked and glowed. A sea-snake in banded yellow sped past and his heart stopped beating as he somersaulted almost on top of a monster, a mottled carcass of dull grey, staring up from bovine eyes. Jack gave himself up for lost. This titanic thing was almost as large as a whale, as long and bigger round than the *Sea Eagle;* he expected its mouth to open and engulf him. He swam weakly towards the surface and the thing followed him, not swiftly but leisurely, a vast bulk arising from the deep. Jack broke surface and screamed, striking out for the canoe. In an instant swimmers were leaping into canoes, hands were clapped underwater to warn those below. Duppa's spear-arm fell as he reached down to grasp Jack and laughed.

"It's all right, Wak, it's only the Father of Sharks." Jack collapsed in the canoe.

"He's too big and sleepy and contented," smiled Duppa. "It is seldom that he hurts a man."

Jack sat up, looked over, and there was the monster, calmly regarding him; Jack shivered, for its great mouth was the length of a man. Shouts of relief went up, a cheer from Bogo, then laughter from the water and from every canoe.

But Jack had got such a fright that he couldn't feel foolish.

15

THE CYCLONE

But the day's work was broken, men lazed indecisively on the canoes. The stupid monster would not go away. Duppa prodded him hard; he only looked surprised and rolled just out of reach. They splashed paddles on the water and shouted at him; he just lay there, half above the surface, gazing at them with amiable stupidity.

"It's not that he's dangerous," explained Duppa to Jack. "The men are uneasy; they sense misfortune since yesterday, and do not care to go down."

"Shall I throw a fish-spear at him?" suggested Jack.

"No. It would not pierce his hide anyway. If it did he might turn on us. Also, if it drew blood it might bring the tigers around. We can only wait until he goes away."

But he wouldn't go. Marboo shouted the order for all canoes to paddle farther along the reef. But immediately the *Sea Eagle* moved, the monster's eyes showed interest; he came along too, quite interested in these strange things that might be some kind of fish.

At last the *War Chief* ceased paddling. Marboo shouted to Duppa to paddle away from die canoes. As the canoe forged away, the great stupid thing followed. Jack would have laughed had he not sensed the worried feeling of all. When a few hundred yards out from the reef the *Sea Eagle* stopped. So did the Father of Sharks and, to Duppa's disgust, stayed beside them all the afternoon while the distant crews worked beside the reef.

Sunset came with a deathly quietness, the sun a ball of fire setting far away over the Great South Land. The *Sea Eagle* paddled back to the canoes. Fires twinkled on the reef, its crown bare with the receding of the tide. The canoes were so loaded now that the crews found it difficult to find standing-room even. They would sail back to Mer loaded deep with good things to help tide the people over the difficult season nearly due.

Stars appeared; the men's low voices sounded unusually distinct. There was not a sound from sea or sky. A fish shot through the water, brilliant as a comet.

"The water must be alive with phosphorus," said Jack.

"Just look down over the reef," answered Bogo.

Jack looked, and saw fairyland in spurts of crimson and green as fish sped by. A cuttlefish shot out from the reef; even that horror looked beautiful.

"It's going to be uncomfortable tonight," said Jack presently. "We're burning the last of our wood too. There's no sand to sleep on here; it will get cold towards dawn."

"Yes," laughed Bogo. "But before then the tide will be in. We'll be squatting out on the canoes hunched up on those shells. But I think the chief will order us to paddle, it will keep us warm; we've got all the shells we want. A couple of days and nights on the dugong grounds and then—up-sail for Mer."

"It's been a wonderful cruise," said Jack, "but I'll be glad to land on Mer again, if only to stretch my legs and sleep warm in Duppa's house."

Around the little fires the crews all stretched out on the rough corals asleep almost as soon as they closed their eyes. Then, when the tide came lapping in they went aboard the canoes and squatted back to back wherever they could, each man's arms around his knees, his head pillowed on his arms.

Jack awoke to a loud bray of the Boo. Sleepily he gazed into utter darkness, then saw Duppa's eyes high by the stern. Duppa grunted urgently, they could not see his outstretched arms. As the Boo brayed again and again, Jack turned and saw far away north a pencil of crimson rising as lightning, though it must have been sixty miles away.

"Gelam!" grunted Duppa.

As they watched, the crimson flamed into vivid green, then turned crimson again.

"The Zogo-le!" said Duppa solemnly. At the dreaded name every man caught his breath. Then the Boo brayed three times, short and sharp.

"Quick!" shouted Duppa, "the Zogo-le has sent word a cyclone is upon us. Overboard with everything."

In an instant frantic men were heaving overboard shells, fish, turtle, birds, everything. Everything they had toiled so hard to win; everything that was to comfort people in the wet season to come. The deathly silence was broken by hundreds of splashes. Jack could have cried at the waste but he worked with the fear that now possessed the flotilla.

Soon the canoes were half unloaded. Then a streak shot through the water, followed by another and another. The sea was beautiful but terrible in fantastic streaks of boiling phosphorus.

"What a shame!" cried Jack. "All we've won, food for the sharks!"

"Hush, lad," grunted Duppa. "We may be food so hasten." And Jack worked in the terrible silence of fear.

Captain after captain shouted his canoe ready. The Boo brayed, the canoes drew close. Impossible to see the *War Chief,* not a star in the sky.

Then the paddles dipped and brilliance in sparkling beauty rose, and dipped and rose as if a many-legged fairy monster was walking upon the sea. Easy to follow each canoe now, for each had grown flaming legs as green phosphorus sparkled from the paddles. Then the canoes shot forward and a streak of boiling green and crimson leaped through the black velvet of the sea.

For hours they sped, driven by tense energy. Dawn should have come—must have come—but yet darkness hung low over all. Then the sky lightened to a black day, a sky of greenish-black, and not a movement. Far away the warning signal died from big old Gelam. The day lightened a little and they sped on, driven by men racing against death. Hours sped by and Mer loomed up, and it was black too. The sea was black glass and deathly quiet; the only sounds the sucking dip of the paddles, the gurgle from bows and outriggers. And in all the sky there was not one bird.

"They've flown to shelter," thought Jack as he strained at the paddle. "They would be blown to sea if they didn't."

The black hump of Mer loomed clearer and Jack saw now how the islanders likened Mer to the long squat bulk of an old bull dugong.

As the paddlers' bent backs lunged forward to strain back, then dip forward again the *Sea Eagle* seemed breathing like a straining animal to the deep breaths of the men. Jack felt his own warm breath labouring out, labouring in; thankful he was for strength and endurance, gained by this hard life. No weakling would have a chance now. He knew that if any man faltered, if any man's heart failed or his wind shortened, the others would throw the gasping wretch into the sea to lighten the canoe. In this race for life every man must pull his weight.

Far behind Gelam a pitch black cloud rapidly formed into a cone reaching heavens high and swiftly bore down upon the extinct crater. Jack thanked God for a racing tide now swiftly rushing them towards the island. The whirling cone was almost upon Gelam. A sudden icy breath swept through the air; men clenched their teeth; then from far away sounded a low moaning. It died away. The great cone spread out wings like a bat to envelop Gelam. A gust of wind came shrieking. It, too, died away. The sea began moving like a lake of glass, under which a giant is slowly awakening from sleep. A low moaning sounded that gradually swelled until it filled the air. The sea broke into little waves, white-capped, a gust came shrieking. Gelam was very near.

"Will we reach it?" thought Jack. "Oh, for just a little more time, a little more strength!"

With sweat pouring from him, though icy air whistled past, he strained at the paddle.

The sea broke into snappy waves; spray dashed past; then came a shrieking as if clouds of demons swept down upon the canoes. Howling wind struck them, icy spray dashed past, the canoes seemed to shiver as they rose and fell to dart ahead. Then waves were breaking, wind howling, sea and air a growing roar of sound. The big bulk of the island blocked the full force of the wind; they would make it just in time. Never though, had they not come racing in with a racing tide behind them.

Through squall gusts Jack got a glimpse of palms swaying in the wind, a black mass of people clinging to the beach. Above an inferno of sound the Death Wail rose faintly as the men now sang. They were telling the people of the deaths of Barza and Tobun; they were forging in to the beach, blinded by clouds of spray and whirling sand. As the canoes dashed far up on the beach, people rushed to them; hands gripped the canoes and ran them far up among the palms. Then through the shrieking wind they rushed into the stockade, tumbling into the shelter of the houses.

The cyclone roared away in twelve hours but the storm lashed the island shores for a fortnight. Driving rain-squalls made all things miserable. Day and night a wild sea thundered against the island shores. Jack was very glad when he could walk out of the village into bright sunlight, a steady nor'-wester churning a still angry sea. He looked upon desolation. Trees lay uprooted; the bushes and grass upon the hillsides were beaten flat; ravines were washed out; huge blocks of coral lay piled upon the once lovely beaches. The island looked like a crouching, half-drowned rat.

Jack realized the wisdom that built the main villages on the sheltered side of the island. He knew he must work harder to live during the nor'-wester season. For storms and violent currents had stirred up the Coral Sea and dirtied the water so that it would be almost useless to dive for shellfish. Divers seldom could see through dirty water.

This rough season also drove most of the fish away, except those that lived in sheltered nooks around the islands and among the reefs. The best fishermen thus had to fish much harder than usual, even to catch a few small fish.

The islanders lived mostly upon what their gardens produced, eked out by what they could win from the sea. They could and still did cruise to adjoining islands, seeking fish. Sometimes the storms and winds and rains would rage for a fortnight. Then bright sunlight would break through the sullen clouds, and every island became alive again as men hurried out with canoe and fish-spear; women hurried to the gardens seeking what scanty produce they could gather. There would be a fortnight of bright weather with choppy seas, then a furious nor'-wester would blow up again. Very cautious were the canoemen of every island. To be caught in a violent nor'-wester with raging currents and tides swirling against one another meant almost certain disaster.

Sometimes three weeks of good weather would be followed by a violent week that kept every fish deep in the sea, every bird in shelter, every human chained to village and hut. But even though voyaging was dangerous, cunning seamen seized their chance to sail the seas; watched for an opportunity to make a lightning raid.

One evening, wet and cold and hungry, Jack returned to his mat in Duppa's hut. There, Marboo the Chief and a Maid-le from the Zogo-house were in earnest conversation with Duppa and Oby.

"Wak," said Duppa solemnly, "we have received word from Eroob that the Aureed skull-hunters have sworn to take your head, and the head of young Ewas. They say it was the presence of Wak the Lamar in the canoe of Duppa that caused them the misfortune of the smashed canoes in the fight during the cruise. They say you two boys still carry a spell of good fortune, and they are going to add your heads to their Zogo-house to transfer the good fortune to them."

Duppa paused. The piercing eyes of the Maid-le were on Jack: "Be ever wary," he cautioned in a deep voice. "It is only by cunning and treachery they can take you. But they will try before this season is over."

16

THE SLEEPERS AT THE GATE

One sunny morning Jack and Bogo marched out with the guards and the women to the gardens. For, though a large island and its warriors greatly feared, life was never quite certain on Mer. Danger might lurk in the small jungle patches along the paths; it might he in wait to spring from the tall grass, or be hiding among the rocks on the headlands.

Night-raiding parties occasionally stole to the island, hid their canoes, crept ashore, and at dawn pounced on any unwary ones. Then they would race to their canoes and be away.

The two boys went on past the gardens and up along a winding path leading around Gelam to the Kwod. Bogo had a message from his father to the Keepers of the Kwod.

On a barren spur running along the edge of Deaudapat the Kwod was hedged in with a thick barrier of bushes. This ground was taboo to all but those with business at the Kwod. This was the young boys' training-ground; they were taken from their parents and trained for their future work in life. And a Spartan training it was. The boys passed a masked guard and entered the Kwod. On a wide stretch of bare ground, like a parade ground, groups of boys were manoeuvring, in squads and circles, under stern-faced teachers. Some were shooting with bow and arrow; some armed with spears charged to a fearsome war-cry; others were learning how to make and handle a harpoon; still others were running steadily or practising various exercises of strength and endurance.

With every mark of respect Bogo approached a war-scarred old warrior and delivered the chief's message. The stem old master grinned broadly and, beckoning to Jack, made him describe the fight of the *Sea Eagle* with the Aureed skull-hunters. With sparkling eyes he listened, then complimented the boys, prophesying they would become warriors of Mer. Bogo left the Kwod with his chest thrown out. Jack felt quite pleased too.

"He's a great old teacher," said Bogo enthusiastically, "but terribly strict. The boys are terrified of him. But when we leave the Kwod we soon learn that his teaching makes men of us."

"It appears to be very strenuous training," said Jack curiously.

"It has to be. You went through it all, but of course you do not remember. Little Ewas will go through it when he grows old enough."

Jack felt sorry at the thought of merry little Will D'Oyly having to go through the Kwod, but knew it must be.

"What happens in the Kwod?"

"Many things, sometimes frightening things. We are first taught endurance, then how to make weapons, then how to defend ourselves, then how to guard against and overcome fear, our worst enemy. One dark night masked men suddenly break into the boys' hut, and with wild yells start thrashing them. Those. who scream and run away have learned nothing. Those who cower silently have learned a little. Those who leap up and fight back have learned their lesson; next day they go to a higher class. The others must go through it all again, until they learn to act and fight against fear."

"It is a cruel way to teach them."

"No," answered Bogo seriously. "It is a good way, and very quick."

"And what is the very last test of all?"

"That depends. For a warrior it is very severe; it is endurance against pain. They stretched me upon an ant-bed, and I never cried out once."

"I would cry out," shuddered Jack.

"You didn't. You went through the test, but you have forgotten. Some boys they thrash with prickly vines. There are different tests. Not all boys go through them. They soon find out the boys best suited to be warriors, those best as fishermen, those best as makers of gardens—and of all else in our life." In the afternoon the two stood on the headland of Gelam-Pit, gazing out to sea. Theirs the duty of watching for fish-shoals, for canoes, for anything which might appear upon the sea.

"It is a clear day," said Jack. "This morning I saw Eroob; it appeared like a cloud on the sea, far away." "Soon the sea mists will come drifting and then we will see only a few miles," answered Bogo lazily. "There you are, away towards the west, a light mist like a wispy cloud drifting over the sea."

The lads had little need to gaze east, for out there rolled the great Pacific. Mer is the farthest eastern island of Torres Strait, near the north end of the Great Barrier Reef. West, north-west and southwest, their eyes patrolled. Mainly west, where lie the many islands of the Coral Sea.

"We can see no island now," mused Jack, "yet we gaze far over the sea. Hard to believe that people can reach here in a night."

"Thinking of your head!" laughed Bogo. "If you lose it, you won't think at all. The skull-hunters can easily come here; it is only a matter of the right time, the right wind, the right tide. At times, swift tides and currents set this way. The raiders come from island to island, taking their time. They wait at the nearest island from here until a favourable wind blows, knowing that by night a strong tide will have set in towards the shores of Mer. They sail, and by sundown are quite near and yet so far away that our look-outs cannot see them. After sundown the tide carries them swiftly towards Mer. They land just before dawn. They hide. And then..."

That very night Jack awoke. It was not the cold hours just before the dawn that awoke him; it was the terrible face of Cut-cut, and gnarled hands reaching for his throat. He choked a scream. Duppa would be hurt if his son woke them all like a frightened girl in the dark! Jack listened. Only his thumping heart and the deep breathing of Duppa and Pamoy. Upon the claypan dull coal still glowed, reflected by the polished eyes of old Duppa-mer stretched to his bamboo frame.

Jack lay back with a sigh of relief. Only a dream. That afternoon's talk with Bogo must have awakened memories of old fears. How terrible if, after all, young Will D'Oyly and he lost their heads to the savages of Aureed! He tried to dismiss the thought. Both he and Will were safe now among the warriors of Mer.

But sleep would not come. He undid the door sheet and peered out. Starlight dimly showed the dark mass of huts, the tips of the stockade, the silhouette of palms against a dull blue sky. Jack crept out and pulled the bark sheet fast behind him. No Lamar spirit should enter Duppa's hut through fault of his. He did not realize how deeply native beliefs were now his beliefs. He went to the stockade gate, resolved on keeping the guard company, lest that nightmare come again.

In the shadows of the stockade dull coals gleamed. Jack stepped up and gazed down on the three guards sitting with their backs to the gate—and asleep.

"Oroto! Tagai! Gobar!" All three asleep.

Jack was amazed at Oroto, a warrior of the Beezam clan, one of Marboo's own men. Jack pictured Marboo coming along now and slitting Oroto's throat. Marboo's rage would overwhelm him; he would not wait to commit these men to the terrible death that awaits Sleepers at the Gate.

Tagai, with his head upon his chest, was snoring softly. Gobar slept with his head lying over on his shoulder, his hands on the ground. Across the open palms lay his club, and long, heavy spear.

Jack liked Oroto, the always smiling Oroto, who had treated him kindly from the first. Tagai too was good-humoured and now and then had taught him tricks in parrying a spear, dodging a club blow. Gobar he disliked intensely; thought him an evil man. But he had always been very kind to young Ewas.

Jack felt almost as angry towards these Sleepers at the Gate as Marboo would have been. These men held the lives of the village in their hands, yet would betray the village for the sake of piggish sleep.

He determined to say nothing but to teach them a lesson they would never forget. Softly he lifted one end of the bottom log which barred the gate, then lifted the other end out of its socket. The tall, narrow gate was now barred by a log across its centre. His strongest efforts could not lift this log clear but he did it by leverage, lowering one end first, then the other. Both logs now lay together on the ground, taken clean out of their sockets. The top portion of the gate was barred by four thick bamboo poles, lashed together. These he managed by levering out one end, then dragging out the other end by help of its own weight. He pulled open the gate.

Panting quietly, he gazed down upon the sleepers. They would awake presently and—the gate would be open!

He smiled at the thought of their blanched faces. They would never know who did it.

He frowned, staring down at Oroto, remembering Oroto's many kindnesses. Jack's mind now knew the native mind; these men would live in a terrible mental misery, imagining some enemy in the village had opened the gate, imagining that enemy feasting on their fears, awaiting day by day that enemy to denounce them. For Sleepers at the Gate that would mean dread vengeance at the hands of Mangur. Jack shivered, for Mangur was Chief of the Secret Society that under the Zogo-le, ruled the island.

No one would denounce these guards. But they would not know that, they would be driven mad by mental fear, would at last commit suicide.

Jack frowned. He noticed the Boo, the alarm-shell of Las. This particular Boo was only used for village alarm; its tone was a piercing blast. He would take the Boo, go a little way, then sit down. Just before dawn he would return. They would have awakened and shut the gate by then surely. He would knock, and whisper he would buy admittance with a —Boo. They would open the gate, he would hand them back the Boo and pass on without a word.

Thus they would know it was he who had opened the gate; and that he would not tell.

17

THE ATTACK

Jack walked out into the night and suddenly felt alone, almost washed he had not left the safety of the stockade. It was chilly too; he was sorry he had left Duppa's warm hut. But he must not return until they had shut the gate—he wondered how long they would sleep. He shivered, then started walking down the path; he would walk to the beach and back again, if only to keep warm.

He walked on, his bare feet making no slightest sound, his bare body merging with the night. He heard the dull murmur of the sea and knew the tide was in.

Starlight gleamed on bush and creeper and silvered the grass upon the little bare crowns of hills. Dense black shadows were the gullies, but black as the pit were the short patches of jungle, through which the path occasionally wound. Jack walked on, ashamed of sudden fear. He was staring, listening intently. His heart began to thump. Then he stepped out of darkness and away below, just off the island shores, saw a little shaft of flame as if burning in among the jagged turrets of a ruined castle. The Sacred Fire this, of the Cult of Waiat. That weird fire always burned. Jack shivered. He wondered what the masked followers of Waiat were doing tonight, hidden deep in the caves and crags of Waiar. Close beside Waiar its fellow island Dauar was a black shadow upon the sea.

As Jack climbed on down the winding path, bushes hid the dread island from sight. Then he stepped into the utter darkness of jungle again, and the silence of a tomb enveloped him. Fireflies glowed and vanished; two terrible eyes ringed with luminous yellow came floating towards him, yellow green ribs floated below the eyes. He sank down; the eyes were almost above him as he rolled from the path. Two more yellow eyes came floating, two more behind them, then two more appeared—his heart thumped madly, as with his mouth pressed to the earth, he peered towards the path. Right past his face the black air seemed moving, then something momentarily shone —the sole of a man's foot!

The legs of men were noiselessly passing. The terrible eyes of Cut-cut were ringed with the yellow-green phosphorus procured from the rotted paste of a fish. This luminous paint glowed upon his ribs. Biskea followed behind and his eyes glowed eerily too.

A raiding party come for him and young Will D'Oyly!

Jack's pounding heart strained almost in relief. This was terror, but not the imaginary terror he had just gone through. He lay there while feet passed by his face; he could not move farther aside for roots and branches. If a foot trod his face he would plunge through the bushes like a terrified animal. But the trained feet of the savages of Aureed trod the centre of the narrow path and did not deviate an inch. And foot after foot, leg after leg passed by.

Suddenly, the awful truth burst upon him. This was not a raiding party come to hide and seek a few heads. This was a war party come to storm Las. And— he had left the gate open!

He almost shrieked at the awful thought of what he had done. As he raised himself to his chest the Boo shell struck his elbow. He clutched it, the blood coursing madly through his veins. Then he plunged straight aside into the jungle with bowed head and thrusting arms, swaying from side to side, as he charged through vine and branch and bush.

Cut and bleeding, he burst through into open grassland and the Boo at his lips brayed frantically in short, sharp blasts that awakened the night. Again and again that Boo brayed, harsh, piercing, urgent. An arrow hissed past his ear, he raced down a gully and up the opposite bank and down again and stood with the Boo raised to the sky. Piercing blasts brayed out into the night. Shadows came leaping down at him, he raced down the gully, then twisted aside and plunged through, bushes into tall grass. And again the Boo brayed madly until the grass swished behind him and he raced for dear life, laughing in wild glee. For the Boo shell of Las was braying, a harsh, deep note rolling over all the island, calling all the villages of Mer to come rushing to the assistance of Las. As he raced he knew he could outwit his pursuers, for he knew every inch of the ground. But they were on the bloodhunt now, and twist and turn as he would, he could not quite shake them off; they were forcing him farther and farther from Las.

Wild shouts came floating towards him, then the deep-throated war-cry of Las echoed by the howl of the Aureed men. Distinctly he heard crash upon crash as he saw the dawn coming. Instinctively then he felt his pursuers had vanished. He sank panting to the grass, listening to Boo shells sounding from all over the island, to shouts of the oncoming men of Zameid, of Sebeg, of Laid. All Mer was a beehive now.

In the cold light of dawn he walked wearily though excitedly back to Las. Had he been in time? He knew he had; the sounds of the fighting told him plainly the warriors had manned the stockade. He sighed in heartfelt relief; but he would never play a practical joke again. He shuddered at thought of what this one had so nearly cost.

From the village came a great hum of excitement, another hum from warriors climbing back up the path. The Aureed men had rushed to their canoes and were now at sea, paddling for their lives. Jack gazed at the crowd at the stockade entrance, at the waving weapons, the excited warriors just appearing up the path. The stockade gate was smashed in, it lay in fragments. But it had held the rush—just long enough.

Cut-cut and a chosen band rushing shoulder to shoulder down the path had hurled themselves at the gate, a living battering-ram. They had leaped back, and charged again and again. Oroto, Tagai, and Gobar were fighting like heroes as the men of Las rushed out to man the stockade.

Outside the stockade lay the bodies of eleven Aureed men. Jack glanced for the bodies of Cut-cut and Biskea. They were not there. A dozen men of Las sat there with busy women attending to their wounds. Children were scrambling to pick up the fallen weapons of the enemy.

Excitedly the people called to him, but they noticed nothing else as he walked to the battered entrance. Oroto, Tagai, and Gobar leaned there, all bloodstained. They stared from terrified eyes, their faces ashen green. Unnoticed by the others, he handed the Alarm Boo of Las to Oroto. Oroto's hand seemed lifeless, he just stared, the three guards stared. Then, smiling as if he had just picked up the Boo, Jack laid it in its accustomed place. At an excited yell he turn as Bogo came running to him.

"Oh, Wak, wasn't it wonderful? What a fight! I missed you in the excitement! You were lucky! You were in the thick of it all! You're smeared with blood but you're not hurt badly. Where were you fighting? At the gate?"

Jack smiled, and told him an imaginary tale. Happily, Bogo was too excited over his own share to take much notice. Excitedly he told of the part he had played.

The Sleepers at the Gate had listened to every word. They looked dully at one another, then crouched down against the stockade, as badly wounded men might do.

Women came hurrying to them, scolding mightily, telling them they knew all the time they were wounded badly. It was no use trying to hide it. Dumbly they shook their heads.

Jack felt very, very glad he had said nothing. These men would never, never sleep at the gate again.

Suddenly Jack stood rock still, realizing the fury of Marboo had he told. The men would have suffered death at the hands of Mangur. But Jack would have earned Marboo's fury too. For—he had opened the gate! He was as guilty as the three guards.

18

TRAGIC NEWS

The pretty little Koko bird in his red and blue coat was calling "ko ko, ko ko," telling the people fine weather had come. Later the little red Berobero bird would arrive, and then the people would know the yams were ready for eating. Jack was glad indeed that the rainy season had again gone by. The sun now shone warmly; the sea grew blue as the currents and storms subsided.

In the now clear water the islanders dived, seeking wealth of the sea. The trees grew new coats, the hillsides turned green under young grass, the gardens grew rapidly. Croton and hibiscus made bright patches amongst tropic flowers that appeared here and there, then burst into colour along every ravine and gully. The sea-birds came in their hosts again; migratory visitors arrived; the island-birds were sweet with song.

The islanders were busy too, straightening houses buffeted by winds, removing fallen trees that blocked the paths, clearing the heaped-up debris and huge blocks of coral thrown on the beaches by tide and storm. Cheerily the crews ran the canoes down to the beaches. Weapons and utensils were spick and span, repaired during the long days when furious rains had kept the people to their houses. Hungry for fresh food, every village on Mer and in all the Coral Sea sprang to active life.

Jack and Bogo joyously launched the *Seagull.* Jack seldom thought of rescue now; he realized that it was rare indeed that a ship was ever sighted from Mer.

He wondered what had become of John Sexton and George D'Oyly. At long intervals he had vaguely heard of them as cruising with the savages among islands far to the west. He supposed that long since this they must have settled down with their supposed parents, just as he and Will had done. Ewas was a full-blown islander now and happy as the day was long. Oby loved him.

One morning while out fishing with Bogo they saw a large canoe approaching from the north.

"The first canoe from Eroob," cried Bogo. "Now we'll hear the news."

Eagerly the men of Mer awaited that canoe, for it brought news of all their world. Many canoes from islands far to the west called at Eroob; seldom at Mer, thus Eroob received news from the Australian coast and right across the Coral Sea to New Guinea. And the people of Eroob relayed the news to Mer.

The. Mamoose received the canoe, and the be-feathered messengers were then led inland to the Zogo-house, for important news must first be told to the Chief Zogo. Then the messengers came down to the main village. People from every village waited there, ready to hurry back to their villages with the gossip.

Part of that gossip shocked and saddened Jack. It was that the Aureed men swore they had killed the two white boys, and added their skulls to the Golgotha on Aureed Island. Ma-am, so they declared, had killed John Sexton, Aboo-yoo had killed George D'Oyly. Furthermore, so Cut-cut swore, sooner or later they would add the heads of Wak and Ewas to those others on Aureed.

Since the failure of the attack on Las they were more than ever determined to do this, being sure now that luck followed the owners of Wak and Ewas. The Eroob messengers added that they were doubtful whether the Aureed men had really killed the two Lamar boys. But they were positive that they would seek the heads of Wak and Ewas, and solemnly warned the two boys and their friends ever to be careful.

Jack was very cast down at this news. Bogo touched him on the shoulder: "It may not be true, Wak," he said softly. "The Aureed men are great liars. The men of Eroob have tried to find out from other natives the truth of this, but in no way can they be certain."

"I hope they are not killed," said Jack. "They are good friends of mine."

"Don't believe it until we have sure news," said Bogo warmly. "The Aureed people would have to seize those boys again before they could kill them. You may be sure the boys' people have looked after them, just as we have looked after you and Ewas."

Jack brightened up, although he never learned for certain that John Sexton and George D'Oyly had been killed. As for himself, he had given up thoughts of rescue.

And yet, thousands of miles away events were slowly moving. Twelve months after the wreck of the *Charles Eaton* the five seamen who had sailed away in the dinghy were rescued from the Malays by the Dutch. And in Batavia their story was taken down by the Dutch Government and forwarded to the British authorities in India.

Of the five men rescued, George Pigott, the bosun, died from wounds and hardship. But Laurie Constantine, Richard Quin, James Wright and Will Gumble survived to tell the tale.

The story as they knew it was printed in the Madras newspapers; then it reached England, and at last Australia, where the forlorn story excited great sympathy in Sydney.

In England an agitation started by William Bayley of Stockton, Middlesex, urged the Admiralty to send out a warship to search for possible survivors. But there seemed such a faint chance after all this time, that the authorities hesitated.

Jack knew nothing of these slowly moving happenings. Besides, he had much to think of in tending Duppa's garden, in watching the Sai, in fishing and cruising, and in attending to the quite numerous duties demanded of every boy.

Young Ewas, ignorant of his past, was quite happy, playing and romping with the village children. He could hurl his reed spears with the best of them and, to Oby's delight, was the best shot of his age with bow and arrow. Oby had spent days in making him his toy weapons, and poddy little Ewas was to be seen every sunny day prowling the beach with baby boys, shooting little fishes, or trying hard to sneak on the long-legged Waru Waru bird as it paddled the beaches.

Young Will D'Oyly how could not speak one word of English; and Jack found, to his utter surprise, that, he was fast forgetting it. Both lads had long been able to speak the language of Mer as if born to it.

And now the Wasikor drums were rumbling; the dull boom of the Nemau drum sounded from the Zogo-house; the time was drawing close for the Bomai Malu ceremonies. In every village, among every clan, men and boys were getting ready their insignias of office, their ceremonial dresses, their badges of degrees.

The Bomai Malu was the most powerful cult in all the islands—in short, a secret society. Under the Zogo-le which ruled all, the chief men of the Bomai Malu had great influence over the lives of the people. Only certain members of certain clans were members of the Bomai Malu. And only men who had climbed higher and higher through initiation after initiation were allowed to the more sacred ceremonies, and the secret councils of the Grand Bomai Malu. Still, those who had passed through a ceremony were expected to see the initiation of others in their turn.

Thus Jack and Bogo were busy bathing, and oiling, and painting their bodies to witness the initiation of the first year initiates.

On the Sacred Grounds was the Malu shrine of giant shells and painted rocks, arranged so that they pointed in different directions of the compass. Each represented a sacred entity, an island, a star, the sea or a season. Thus the sea, the earth, and all above the earth, so far as the islanders knew, were represented.

Armed guards of the Gelar patrolled the grounds guarding the ceremonies from unwanted eyes. The Kesi, the initiates a year younger than Jack and Bogo, stood very silently in a large horseshoe line. The Kesi boys of the Beizam boai clan had their arms painted red, with a scarlet band painted down the face, and a red cross below the chest, with a scarlet pendant upon the chest. Each wore a Kus belt, brilliant in coloured seeds and shells and corals. From the carefully prepared hair of each stood up a Daumer lub, a black-tipped white feather of the Torres Strait pigeon. The stem of the feather was split and this caused a rapid vibration from the slightest air current, or even from the breathing of the boys, so that a soft whirring sound was continually rising amongst them.

From the Sacred House six men now advanced towards the initiates: three of the Beizam boai, followed by three of the Zagareb-le. These men were painted all over a bright red, and each was clad in a neat apron of silvery si leaves. Their feathered headdresses were magnificent. The Beizam carried the sacred masks of polished tortoise-shell as tall as a man, painted and befeathered and decorated with many coloured symbols, each of which held a meaning. Jack had seen many masks, but none so impressive as these. He listened eagerly as the Zagareb-le began to sing the story of Bomai and Malu.

"These lads are only the Meket siriam," said Bogo. "You and I have gone through their initiations. But next year," he added eagerly, "we are to become members of the Ume-le—the men who know.

"These initiations go on for years," continued Bogo. "We who are patient and gain the knowledge pass degree after degree until at last we rule Mer. That is," and he lowered his voice, "the Zogo-le rule Mer, and all. But after the Zogo-le comes Mangur our great master. Through him we, after the Zogo-le, rule Mer, and Eroob and Ugar, and even make our power felt far across the Strait."

"There must be some not eligible, and many who do not go through all the degrees," commented Jack.

"Of course. Many are satisfied to be just of us. It is only a few among us who rise up until we guide the destinies of all."

"After the Zogo-le?" smiled Jack.

"Of course—after the Zogo-le,"

The ceremonies lasted many days, taking place in various shrines in secluded places all over the island. But only those with business were admitted to each ceremony.

The initiation of the young lads occupied two days, after which they were drawn up before the chiefs and their fathers, and gravely told that they were no longer boys. They could not play about now as boys; they must begin to work as men. Their days must no longer be spent in fishing on the reefs; each must start a garden and cultivate it. The sea was very good, fish and fishing were very good. But the sea was treacherous; its seasons uncertain. Some seasons brought plenty of fish, other seasons brought a scarcity.

But the garden of Mother Earth bore fruit always if only man would work the ground. They were advised to start a garden, to plant coconuts and bananas, yams and sugar-cane and tobacco; to build a strong house for themselves and fence it with tall bamboos to protect it against the winds. Much good advice was tendered them.

And then, but with terrible earnestness, it was impressed upon them all that to tell one secret told them about Bomai and Malu, meant—death.

In silence they listened yet again while it was impressed upon them that the betrayal of a secret would mean Mangur and death.

"Come on," whispered Bogo, "let's walk. That's the worst of it," he said glumly, "all those instructions about the gardens. It's true enough; but canoe work and fishing and turtle-hunting and dugong-hunting are far more interesting. The old men know we will soon learn all there is to know about fishing, for we love it. But not many of us love gardening. Look at your garden and mine!"

"They're not bad," laughed Jack. "But we'd go hungry if we had to depend on our gardens alone."

"Luckily, we don't," laughed Bogo. "We're too good with the spear and harpoon; we can buy lots of the fruit we need. But let us hurry back to Las; old Ramo is making me a coronet of lovely feathers for the dance."

"Just as well old Ramo loves the sea crayfish more than the banana and yam," smiled Jack.

"Why?" asked Bogo in surprise.

"Because otherwise he would be making a coronet for some lad who grows a good garden."

Again Bogo laughed. "Of course he would. I never thought of it that way. It's a good job that all men have not the same tastes."

Along every village path women and girls were carrying great bunches of bananas and fruits and vegetables to the cooking-fires outside the villages. For this season of plenty was given up to the ceremonies, to feasting and dancing.

19

THE RACE TO SAVE THE FLEET

There was great activity now on Mer, refitting and provisioning the big trade canoes. For this was the season when the traders of Mer, Eroob, and Ugar islands sailed to New Guinea to trade. Men among the clans on each island who were keen traders were held responsible for the business. Several traders were allotted to each canoe.

Every season, Mer and Eroob provided a large flotilla, Ugar a smaller one. The flotillas combined and when they sailed from Ugar they were a fleet heavily manned with fighting-men. For though each season's trade was transacted peacefully, still the fleet must pass by many islands and, especially when they reached the New Guinea shores, much country held by many thousands of would-be pirates. These, when they felt brave enough, would combine and form an ambush amongst the islands, or attack the returning fleet on some jungle-clothed river.

But the war canoes of the islanders were far bigger and stronger than those of the attackers, and the islanders were better fighters, better organized, better armed. Their fleet sailed together and, skilfully led, had always managed to break through when attacked. When they reached New Guinea shores they were outnumbered by fifty to one, still in case of attack it was their leaders who had the brains. And numbers don't count against brains.

Still, there had been some great battles between the trading fleet and the countless canoes of the savages that thronged the great waterways of New Guinea. To the lads who were just about to become men their keenest desire was to be picked to sail with the trading fleet.

Bogo was broken hearted, for the Mamoose had ordered Marboo the Chief to stay behind and guard the welfare of Las. But Duppa and his canoemen were among the chosen, and Jack was to sail with them. At the last moment Bogo entreated his father to allow him sail in the *Seagull* with the fleet as far as Eroob, there with Erubian friends to await the return of the fleet. And Marboo consented.

After a farewell feasting and the blessing of the Zogo-le the fleet sailed to a great blare of Boo shells. And next day reached Eroob. Duppa was immediately called before the Zogo-man of Eroob.

The old warrior returned from the Zogo-house with troubled brow and walked slowly down to the beach at Medigee Bay. There, he laid his hand on Jack's shoulder.

"Wak," he said, "you must stay behind on Eroob. Word has come that the New Guinea men-swear to add your head to the stuffed heads in their Dubu houses."

"But why should they want my head? They are people far away; I have never seen them, never done them any harm."

"They still believe you a Lamar, Wak; you are white to them and your head is white—very valuable. Cut-cut has been to New Guinea where at a great price, one by one, he has traded a few heads of the Lamars, your ship mates. And he has told the New Guinea men that possession of you would bring great luck. The Zogo-le have guessed that that luck means the taking of the fleet. And the Zogo has ordered that you stay behind."

Jack knew there was no appeal; he turned to the sympathy of Bogo. The fleet sailed and the two boys were consoled by old Ag-ghe. Ewas was on Eroob, too, with Oby who often travelled between Eroob and Mer. Oby had a little plot of ground on Eroob which a kinsman worked on the half-share system. Little Ewas was nearly as well known here and as much a favourite as he was on Mer.

The two boys had a cheery time for several weeks, visiting village after village. Then they started sailing around the island shores, the *Seagull* the envy of the boys and young men. But stem work lay ahead. One night the lads were awakened, to look into the solemn face of the Mamoose. Jack shivered, for beside him stood a Maid-le, a sorcerer. On his brow and chest was painted the scarlet triangle which marked him a flying messenger of the Zogo-le.

"Listen," said the Mamoose earnestly, "the Maid-le, on business of the Zogo-le, must reach Maubiag Island with all speed. Yours is the fastest canoe in all the Coral Sea. Hasten! Throw in food and a bamboo of water, and put to sea!"

The boys snatched their weapons, silently the four left the house heavily loaded with food and water: They ran the canoe to the beach. The Mamoose glanced at the Maid-le. He nodded.

Then the Mamoose turned to the boys. "The men of Moa and Badu talk of making peace, of joining forces and attacking the Maubiag people, our friends, if they do, it will be the signal for war right across the Strait. Our trading fleet will never come back. The Maid-le goes to warn the people of Maubiag. If he can do so in time, it will stop the big outbreak. Your little canoe may get through where a war canoe would not only be seen but would start the war. If you reach Maubiag in time you save our trading fleet. If not, you need never come back. Go!"

They pushed off the *Seagull.* Jack leaped to the sail, Bogo to the steering-oar and sought a star west of south, a dull red star that shone directly over the island of Damuth. He steered the *Seagull* by the star, speeding the sail by knowledge of tide and currents. Hours wore by. Jack constantly trimmed the sail to catch every strength of the wind. The canoe skimmed over the water and Jack crept away out on to the outrigger to windward and lay there lest the *Seagull* capsize. He thrilled to the slippery grip, to the vibration of the racing canoe. Black water rushed past his nose, hissed like steam as the outrigger float skimmed through it. If he slipped or was washed off they would leave him there, he knew, but the skill necessary to balance the flying canoe thrilled him through and through.

And—they were racing to save the fleet. He knew what Bogo must feel: if they reached Maubiag in time the Zogo-le would grant him his warrior-hood and his story would be sung in dance and play-acting through all, the years to come.

The boys did not speak for they were overawed by the presence of the Maid-le. He crouched in the canoe, his eyes glowing, his sombre mouth tight shut. The dread insignia of the sorcerer gleamed dully on brow and breast. This man would be feared no matter where he went; even hostile tribes would dread him. But he knew that if he failed to reach Maubiag in time he dared never return to face the wrath of the Zogo-le.

Just before dawn the canoe ran up the beach at Damuth. They leaped out, surprised at fires burning before the village, black shapes of excited warriors, hum of voices rising to angry shouts.

A death-like silence greeted their appearance. The Maid-le of Damuth, evil looking with his one eye and necklace of human teeth, instantly arose and hurried towards the fateful messenger. The two sorcerers conversed in low, hurried tones.

Jack's heart beat fast as a huge form strode forward and there glared down at him the ferocious face of Cut-cut. He reached out a great paw as Jack jumped back, while Bogo stepped forward with an arrow to his bow. As Biskea leaped beside Cut-cut both men raised a shout and rushed towards the boys with swinging clubs. A yell held Bogo's arrow to its bow, Cut-cut's club poised on high, as the Maid-le of Damuth sprang towards them. Furiously he spoke, while a dozen Aureed men silently stepped beside Cut-cut and Biskea.

The giant chief wheeled around and waving his club harangued the Damuth men.

"We want the heads of Wak and Bogo. We mean to take them. Do you sit there like women when but a moon ago your men fell to the spears of the men of Mer?"

A low muttering arose, an uneasy shuffling for weapons. Then the

Maid-le of Eroob strode into the firelight. They saw the scarlet triangle upon his chest and brow. Under his malevolent eyes deathly stillness reigned; no man there dared question the authority of a messenger of the Zogo-le. Cut-cut frowned, his handful of Aureed men stared sullenly.

"Come!" snapped the sorcerer. And he and the Maid-le stepped out into the darkness, the boys at their heels. Once in the darkness they breathed again.

"A narrow escape, Wak!" whispered Bogo.

"I thought my head was gone," whispered Jack.

"But what could have happened to make the men of Damuth so angry? They are friendly to the men of Eroob, and are not at war with us."

"Something serious is doing among all the islands. We must race to Maubiag, Bogo, and save the fleet. If we don't—we will never get back."

"We'll save the fleet!" said Bogo huskily—then an arrow hissed past his ear.

The four were instantly on their knees and wheeling around glared into the darkness. There was nothing to be seen, except away back among the trees the dull glow of fires.

"Come!" hissed the sorcerer. They launched the canoe. There was something so evil in that hiss that Jack shuddered. He could only guess at what would happen to Cut-cut and Biskea should ever they fall into the hands of the Zogo-le.

The *Seagull* left the Maid-le of Damuth standing like a shadow on the beach. A worried Maid-le with a rebellious people upon his hands, and with strict orders, too, from the Zogo-le to force his people to do what they would not like. He turned towards the fires. He would immediately invite Cut-cut and his Aureed desperadoes to leave the island. If they did not, he would order his men to kill them. If they refused... Frowning, he rushed back into the firelight spilling his orders in a furious torrent of words in the name of the dreaded Zogo.

Meanwhile, the canoe raced out to sea. "Maubiag!" snarled the messenger. Bogo swung the canoe towards the distant isle.

A sudden exclamation from Jack and they stared at a fire signal arising from Damuth.

Cut-cut and his men, sullenly making for their canoe, had fired the island to warn all of their coming.

The Maid-le ground his teeth. He knew what the boys did not know. That the trading fleet in passing this way had had a quarrel forced upon them by the Damuth men. Three Damuth men had been killed. The quarrel had been patched up, an uneasy peace made.

But what troubled the Maid-le was that a friendly island behind him was now half enemy. Between him and Maubiag lay a hundred islands simmering on the brink of war, a war which if started by the great islands of Moa and Badu would mean a united attempt to break up the power of the Zogo-le. Let one spark start it before he could reach Maubiag and it might well mean the end. He stared ahead while the red glow from Damuth spread higher into a lightening sky.

The Augud trophy with the skulls of those that survived the shipwreck of the Charles Eaton.

20

WAR

All that day the canoe raced west never out of sight of an island; most were inhabited. Distantly they sometimes saw large canoes, apparently fishing upon the reefs, but no canoe gave chase. But, as they passed, from island after island a smoke coiled up. This was the race of Bogo's life. Should he misjudge position by sun or tide or current, reef or shoal or wind, they would be thrown miles out of their course and would be too late. Jack needed all his endurance now in balancing the canoe as it tore through the water under a stiff breeze; By late afternoon the big peak of Moa loomed above the sea. Jack, lying stretched on the outrigger, stared at that massive peak, wishing he could visit the island with a strong force of men from Mer.

Moa and Badu are the main islands of the western group, as Mer and Eroob were the chief islands of the eastern group. Moa and Badu were often at war. But if these two great islands combined and defeated Maubiag they would swing all the islands between Moa and Damuth against Mer and Eroob—and the Zogo-le.

Sundown came with the hills of Badu turning pink upon a crimson sea. The peak of Moa seemed to loom over Badu as the canoe sped on. Maubiag was not far away. Night came, and suddenly the Maid-le hissed. Dark forms of war canoes were coming behind.

Bogo laughed in sheer delight. They could never catch the *Seagull.*

Stars shone out of a dark sky then a half moon appeared, dimmed by fleecy clouds. The Maid-le snarled like a trapped animal. In crescent shape ahead canoes were bearing down upon them; Jack saw the gleam of moonlight upon the mat sails. There was no escape.

"A trap!" snarled the Maid-le. "Quick, overboard! while they are still not close enough to see. If I return, send me a snake from any island. I'll see whether these dogs ahead dare stop a messenger of the Zogo-le!"

Quietly the boys slid overboard while the canoe sped on.

"Float," whispered Bogo, "with only nose above water until we hear them coming. Then sink. Be careful when you rise, or you may be seen from slower canoes behind the leaders."

Jack floated, grasping his spear and bow. His dagger and arrows were girdled around him. Soon he heard a gurgle from a rapidly advancing canoe. Slowly he sank, and the black bottom of the canoe glided overhead. Presently he rose but quickly sank as another canoe came hissing by. He rose again. Then raised his head and listened ... to the sound of canoes drawing away. Bogo came gliding towards him.

"Why did he make us go overboard?" exclaimed Jack. "He has no chance."

"A good chance," said Bogo confidently. "Those canoes ahead were only from small island tribes. They will be too frightened to stop a messenger of the Zogo-le. But had we been with him they would have closed in to take our heads, or would have held us up long enough for the war canoes of Moa to come up. Those warriors would not have hesitated to kill us—and the Maid-le too. They've been worked up to it. As it is, the Maid-le will sail straight through the small people and on to Maubiag."

"Twice in a few hours we've had a narrow escape," said Jack.

"Worse than that," answered Bogo gravely. "If the men of Moa had killed the Maid-le, word of it would have sped from island to island. Every hand would have been raised against Mer and Eroob."—Bogo sank before Jack's eyes.

Jack stared, then suddenly dived straight down behind Bogo's struggling form. In the dark twilight below Bogo, two fiendish eyes glared up, two sinewy hands gripped Bogo's heels. Jack whipped out his long bone dagger and, turning as a shark turns, plunged the dagger into a muscular back. He felt a violent lunge; saw Bogo's feet shooting up; shot up himself.

Bogo was gasping on the surface. Panting, they glared around, listening.

There came a faint noise.

"Quick!" whispered Bogo. "Swim quietly; there are others."

For a mile the boys were carried quietly along by a swift current. Then Bogo sighed and laughed softly.

"Wak, I owe my life to you."

"Forget it. You saved me from the shark."

Bogo smiled.

Presently Jack asked: "Why didn't he knife one of us?"

"Because he feared the living one would then kill him," answered Bogo fiercely. "So he just grabbed my heels and jerked me down. He reckoned you would have" suspected sharks. Later he would swim after you, come up below you, and thus get both of us."

Jack shuddered. "Bogo, I really did think it was a shark—or a giant groper."

"But you came down after me all the same."

"How did he come to be there?" asked Jack.

"They guessed what had happened, so a few dived overboard to make sure. They expected the *Seagull* would be stopped by the canoes ahead, so they could easily swim after them."

"The man who tackled us must have heard us talking."

"Of course. A man every here and there slipped overboard and slowly swam after the canoes, listening as he swam. They knew we'd start talking as soon as the canoes had passed."

"What do we do now?"

"Let the current carry us along; it will swing in against an island sooner or later. There we can hide if no one sees us, and watch out until we see the Maid-le returning."

"What if we miss him?"

"We'll have to steal a canoe and make a dash for Eroob."

"I wonder if he got through?"

"I'm sure he did; war hasn't started yet. Those small people dare not stop a messenger of the Zogo-le. But they would have held him back until the Moa war canoes came up had we been with him."

The swim was easy, the boys mostly floated on their backs, helping the powerful current with a guiding kick now and then. Their weapons were little trouble for these floated too. And the water was warm, buoyant with playful waves. Jack gazed up at the stars, thankful that he could now float and swim for hours. He hoped the Maid-le had got through. He had no need to think of food or clothes, of shelter or help. They would win their own food, while a cranny in the rocks or a hide-out in the scrub would be shelter enough. He only occasionally felt the need of clothes in this warm season of the year. All that the boys need fear were men enemies, and these they must outwit.

Just before dawn Bogo said: "Listen! do you hear that?"

They trod water, listening above the swirl of the waves.

"Yes," said Jack presently, "the sea breaking on a reef."

"Turtle Back Reef," said Bogo. "It always sings like that in quiet weather. Kos Island is nearby and no one lives there. There is a spring on it so we'll have water. Swim now and we'll make the island before dawn."

A beautiful dawn, the sun a golden ball just peeping above the rim of the sea as the boys waded ashore.

It was a tiny, barren island, little more than a pile of rocks on a long sand-mound upon which grew a small but thick patch of scrub. Elsewhere, the isle was dotted with shaggy trees, bushes, and vines. An encircling reef protected it from the sea. An uninviting spot, castaways would have perished there. But to the boys it meant a haven of shelter, water, and food. They stepped and jumped from stone to stone, so as not to leave tracks should any prowling canoes visit the islet, then dived into the scrub.

"First, we make a fire," said Bogo, "and dry our bowstrings. We can then start a signal-fire by night, or a smoke by day to guide the Maid-le. Look around for tinder, Wak, while I find the fire-sticks."

Jack collected dry, fluffy bark and shredded it, while Bogo soon returned with two very light, fibrous, dry sticks. He bent down and vigorously began sawing one stick against the other. In a surprisingly short time the under stick began to faintly smoulder. Bogo sawed swift and hard and a faint puff of smoke arose; sawed with all his speed and the stick smouldered noticeably; blew the stick vigorously and tiny sparks appeared. Thrusting the stick amongst the grass tinder he blew hard; a tiny flame leaped up, then the tinder caught alight. They fed it with dry sticks.

"It's right," said Bogo finally. "The log is catching now, it will smoulder and throw out warmth without smoke."

"The bushes will hide any little smoke," said Jack.

"Yes. Now, lay your bow fairly close, beside mine. The strings will soon dry."

"It's a good job the strings are from the skin of bamboo, and not animal sinew," said Jack.

"If they were sinew," said Bogo, "we'd be without weapons, except for our spears. Come on, we'll find the spring."

Taking a fire-stick, they walked through the bushes and out on to a little grassy flat in the centre of the islet. By the base of some rocks was a mound of sand surrounding a small circular hole. Birds fluttered up, scolding the boys, as Bogo glanced over at the water.

"It's all right," he said. "Someone has dug the spring out only a few days ago. Now we'll climb these rocks and glance out to sea; the sun is well up. Don't show yourself until we're sure no one is upon the sea."

Cautiously climbing, they peered out over the trees at a rosy sea fast turning into silver.

"Not a sail anywhere," said Bogo. "But let us go to the top and make sure."

There they peered out over the sea, to the horizon all around.

"Not a sign of a canoe," declared Bogo. "Not even towards Moa and Badu."

"The Peak of Moa looks very close," said Jack, "yet it must be some miles away. You'd never think those hills of Moa and Badu were on separate islands."

"No," said Bogo, "but they are. The waterway dividing them is only a mile wide. I've visited there only once, and then with my father. The men of Mer are not welcomed by those of Moa and Badu."

"Just as well; they are always: fighting against each other", said Jack. "Those two big islands must swarm with warriors."

"They're alive with fighting-men," answered Bogo grimly. "And it is fortunate for Maubiag that they fight one another. Maubiag sometimes helps Badu against Moa, just to keep things going. Hence, Badu does not attack Maubiag, and Moa cannot, for Moa is kept busy with Badu. But if Moa and Badu combine..."

"I suppose the Zogo-le's plan is to warn Maubiag," said Jack, "so that Maubiag will hurry its war canoes across to Badu and suggest an attack on Moa."

"Of course. It keeps the balance."

"Mer and Eroob would look small beside Moa and Badu."

"Yes. Our islands are the largest in the east but they are small compared to those in the west. But size matters nothing," added Bogo proudly; "it is the wisdom of men that counts. And the wisdom of the Zogo-le has kept these great peoples from our throats since ever Man came here. And will beat them every time... He got through! I am sure of it. Otherwise the combined-fleets of Moa and Badu would be sailing to attack Maubiag—we wouldn't see the water for canoes. Had they killed the Maid-le it would have been the signal for attack."

Jack turned and pointed north-east: "What are those islands away out there?"

"Sassie," pointed Bogo, "Turtle Back, Yamar, Maquar, Jeaka, and those clouds on the sea, so far away, are islands stretching all the way from here to Eroob, and from here to Mer. You have visited most of those when you lived with the skull-hunters of Aureed. You have visited others in our cruises from Mer."

"This is a sea of islands and reefs."

"Yes. In songs of Mer we call it our 'sea of islands'."

A sudden faint but agitated booming caused them to turn.

"War drums!" gasped Bogo. "Listen!"

Now, carried to them by a growing breeze, came unmistakably the deep, growling boom of drums of war. From the tallest hill of Maubiag arose a rolling column of dense smoke, answered by a column from the hills of Badu.

"Maubiag and Badu in alliance," shouted Bogo in ecstasy. "Watch the Peak of Moa! Watch keenly brother Wak!"

Even as he spoke there arose from the towering peak a rolling column of smoke as if in haughty defiance. War drums boomed harshly.

"Moa accepts the challenge!" danced Bogo. "Maubiag and Badu are at war against Moa. We have saved the fleet!"

21

THE LAST STAND

They stared, watching the rising smoke, listening to the drums.

"If Badu and Maubiag war against Moa," said Jack at last, "it means that not only the trading fleet is safe, but that Mer and Eroob are secure against attack."

"Of course," laughed Bogo. "The Zogo-le have set them against one another again. Otherwise they would have overwhelmed Maubiag, then sailed to attack Eroob, collecting all the little peoples as they sailed. All would have hurried to join the combined fleets of the two big victors; a swarm from all the island sea would have attacked Eroob. Had they overwhelmed it, then they would have come swarming to Mer."

"Just as well the Maid-le got through!" said Jack grimly.

"Just in time," laughed Bogo. "They would have attacked Maubiag in hours. If not, why did those war canoes try to intercept us last night?"

"Hadn't we better find something to eat," suggested Jack. "We want strength soon."

Bogo could hardly tear himself away. "Good advice", he admitted unwillingly. "We must eat, but we may see the *Seagull* soon now—the Maid-le will be in haste to report to Eroob. We will light the smoke-signal up here now so he can sail straight to us."

"Hadn't we better wait," suggested Jack, "until we sight the canoe."

"No, no. There is no danger now; every island will be too interested in the happenings on Moa and Badu and Maubiag. Come, the *Seagull* sails swiftly. Let us light the signal then fish and eat before she comes."

Quickly they whirled the fire-stick into flame, built a fire and, when it was burning fiercely, threw on green bushes. Then they picked up their spears and hurried to the reef. Soon they had speared a dozen fish, and hurrying back to their bows and arrows in the scrub, threw the fish on the coals.

"The bowstrings are dry," said Bogo. "It must be awful to lose your weapons."

"It looks now as if we won't have to use ours this time."

"You never know," said Bogo. "This fish is good."

It was an excited breakfast, with a growing breeze carrying the throb of distant drums to their ears. A sea eagle sailed high in the sky.

"An omen!" laughed Bogo as he pointed to it. "The totem bird of your father's war canoe."

"Let us hope he also finds good fishing," said Jack, "and enjoys his breakfast as much as we. Will they be fighting on Moa and Badu now?"

"Only across the waterway; light canoes challenging one another. The big fighting won't be for a few days, not until the canoes of Maubiag arrive in force at Badu. They'll sail to-day, we may see them from the rocks above when we finish breakfast."

"The Moa warriors will be angry at the treachery of Badu."

"They will fight all the more fiercely," laughed Bogo. "Our Maid-le must have acted swiftly and surely."

"The Zogo-le are very cunning," said Jack thoughtfully.

"They are trained to it in the Councils. They know every people in the Strait; all their war and trade, all their quarrels over fishing rights and land rights; they know their allies and enemies, all their hates and fears. Thus they play one people against the other, tribe against tribe. Thus Badu and Moa have never spread right across to the east—fortunately for us."

"The Zogo-le were nearly tricked this time," said Jack.

"Very, very nearly; only a matter of hours. But come, let us climb up on to the rocks, and throw more bushes on the fire."

Jack was just picking up his weapons when he saw a savage face peering from behind a tree. "Quick," he hissed.

The face vanished as Bogo jumped back into the bushes.

"What was it?" he whispered.

"A savage! one of the small people. He wore a crane's feather with yellow paint across his forehead."

"Karraweid men," exclaimed Bogo in disgust. "What a miserable end should we now fall to them! How many did you see?"

"Just the one."

"It may be only one canoe load," said Bogo hopefully, "a fishing-canoe perhaps."

"We're cornered," said Jack grimly.

"Not yet. We'll crawl through the bushes and find their canoe. Be careful, but shoot if you get a chance; every man hit means a man less when the rush comes."

Silent as snakes they wormed their way through the undergrowth—the only sound the twittering of a bird. Yet savages lay hidden around them trying to find just where they were.

As they crawled they peered to the right and left, pausing again and again to peer cautiously behind.

"The vines are too thick for an arrow shot," whispered Bogo. "They'll try and surround us—then rush. Quick—let's find the canoe."

They did. Peered through the bushes near the island shore and saw the canoe out near the reef edge—with two savages guarding it.

"We must fight," whispered Bogo. "It is open ground between here and the canoe; they would shout before we could reach them. Creep back to the rocks, that's where we must fight."

They wormed their way back, neither seeing nor hearing any sign of man. Evidently, the savages were puzzled at finding no canoe; they could not guess how many men might be hidden in the scrub or amongst that big mound of bush-sheltered rocks.

"When they come," whispered Bogo, "shoot straight. We may have a chance. There can be only eight men ashore, that fishing-canoe would not hold more."

They ducked as a heavy spear came plunging through the bushes.

They crouched, staring through the vines with arrows fitted to bows. But the unseen spearman was silent as they.

Inch by inch Bogo crawled beside Jack, then bent his lips to his ear.

"Crawl softly ahead," he whispered. "When you are about twenty feet ahead make a careful, rustling noise."

Jack nodded and moved ahead inch by inch.

Bogo waited, an arrow fitted to his bow. Presently, there sounded a rustling of bushes as if a man were crawling away. Instantly there arose a feathered head, two gleaming eyes peering from a band of yellow.

Then the feather bobbed down as the wearer started to crawl forward on hands and knees. Bogo could just see the tip of the advancing feather. Drawing a deep breath, he slowly pulled back the bowstring.

Again came that rustling and the savage's head immediately popped up to full view.

"Twang!" and the savage writhed to earth with an arrow through his throat.

Almost instantly Bogo was beside Jack: "One less!" he hissed excitedly. "I got him! If we can get a few more like that and not get shot ourselves we'll win out. Keep your wits about you. Creep forward to the rocks."

They got right to the base of the rocks, now looming above them. Bogo pointed up: "See that big rock near the top, the rock that leans right out like a house?"

"Yes."

"Well, that rock will shelter us from attack above us. They can't take us from behind or above. We will shelter among the rocks below the overhanging rock, and fire down at them."

"A great idea", agreed Jack. "They can shoot at us from only one way and even then we've got the shelter of the rocks."

"That's it. Now pick out the two rocks you are going to squeeze between. Then, we must run for life, leap from rock to rock, then jump in between the rocks and turn and shoot."

"I'm ready," whispered Jack.

Both lads leaped for the rocks. It was easy. They were almost up to the leaning rock when a wild yell rang out below. As Jack jumped to his new position a hastily-aimed arrow hissed by; two more followed the triumphant cry of Bogo. Jack squeezed down between the rocks with bowstring half drawn. He aimed and let fly at two wild, figures below but missed. He heard the twang of Bogo's bow, and fitted another arrow as six arrows came sailing up. He fired again as the savages vanished. He was bitterly disappointed.

"Save our arrows!" called Bogo. "Only shoot when you're sure."

"I've only eight arrows left," said Jack seriously.

"And I've seven," answered Bogo cheerily. "That's plenty. There are only seven men now against us, so long as the other two stand by the canoe. Make it a long, careful fight. Time is on our side. Protect yourself carefully; there are plenty of loose stones you can build around you."

"Can you see any of the arrows they fired?" asked Jack.

"Yes, three, but they're no good, the points have broken against the rocks."

Jack stared down at the little scrubby patch below realizing how excellently Bogo had chosen in making this their last stand. Except in one long narrow place, the undergrowth down there was separated from the rocks by open ground, growing coarse tufts of grass here and there. No man could cross from the scrub to the rocks without being seen. From the centre of the scrub, a thin line of undergrowth ran nearly to the edge of the rocks. It was under shelter of this that Bogo and Jack had reached the rocks. But that line of undergrowth stretching out from the scrub was so narrow that it could not give cover to more than two men abreast.

"If they rush out of the scrub, we must get four of them when they're climbing up towards us," said Jack.

"And that will leave only two of them, if they dare come on."

"They wouldn't," laughed Jack. "We've a great chance."

"If we only shoot straight."

The boys waited, while invisible eyes below searched them out. Though they could not see the boys, the savages now knew exactly where they were. But no arrow could reach them while they kept hidden thus... Time dreamed on. The sea eagle still circled in the sky.

"He's watching over us," smiled Bogo. "Didn't I tell you the totem bird of our clan is a good omen?" —and just then a rock crashed beside his head.

"Are you hurt?" cried Jack.

"No," answered Bogo angrily. "Serve me right if I was. They were listening to us talking. Several must have climbed up behind us and are lying on the rock above. One man leaned over and hurled the stone in under here. They won't do it that way a second time. Presently, those in the scrub below will yell and rush out on to the cleared places. But don't waste an arrow for they will run back. The men above will think we're firing at those below. They'll lean out over this boulder then, and throw rocks at us."

"A clever idea," said Jack.

"Not so clever," answered Bogo grimly, "if I can only send an arrow through a face. But it will be a quick difficult shot. You help me. As soon as they run out of the scrub below you shout: 'Here they come! Here they come!' But keep your head well down."

"You bet I will," smiled Jack. "Here they come!" he shouted excitedly. "Look out! They really are!" as with a wild scream five men dashed out of the scrub with arrows fitted to bows. Yelling war-cries they leaped in the air as they advanced. Out of the corner of his eye Jack saw two savage heads suddenly peer down over the overhanging boulder, and a rock came whizzing in as Bogo's bowstring twanged. There was a shriek, a slowly sliding body, then a savage dived head-first, an arrow through his eye.

As he crashed to the rocks, Bogo shouted in triumph, echoed by Jack's shout of congratulation. In their excitement they did not notice the sudden silence. The savages had vanished. Then they saw the Maid-le.

He stood there in a cleared patch, gazing up. Silent, they stared. He beckoned.

"Come," said Bogo. They crawled from the rocks, climbed down, and walked straight out to the Maid-le. Not an arrow was fired.

"Eroob!" said the Maid-le, "and swiftly." He turned and they followed him. The *Seagull* was drawn up near the savages' canoe. The two men guarding it crouched there silently.

"Not a man in the Strait," thought Jack in awe, "dare touch a painted messenger of the Zogo-le. It is well to be a man of Mer."

They pushed the *Seagull* off, stepped into her, and set sail for distant Eroob. And the wind followed them, carrying with it the dull throb of war drums away behind.

22

A SHIP! A SHIP!

The next day at sunset the flying *Seagull* arrived at Eroob to a great reception; even the grim figures of the Zogo-le stood a little apart, waiting. The Mamoose and all the chiefs seized the *Seagull* and carried it shoulder high up the beach and into the very centre of the cheering crowd. The Maid-le slipped away with the Mamoose to report to the Zogo-le.

The chiefs and warriors crowded around Bogo and Jack, eager for news of the great events in the west. They could not answer questions quickly enough. Fires were lighted on the beach; a feast was spread; they talked far into the night.

Quickly, a canoe was launched and manned while the people were feasting, and the Maid-le lay down in the canoe and fell fast asleep. That man had not closed his eyes since the *Seagull* left Eroob.

The canoe sped away towards Mer. There, the Maid-le would report to the Chief Zogo, at the Chief Lodge of the Zogo-le. Only then would his duty be finished.

Jack and Bogo found themselves the heroes of Eroob, and of Mer. They had saved the trading fleet.

But the Zogo-le had saved Eroob and Mer.

A week later and the Maid-le returned from Mer. And presently the Mamoose came down from the Zogo-house and sent a messenger to every village on Eroob. Three days later a great concourse of people gathered on the beach at Medigee Bay. Then the Mamoose stepped forth and in a deep rolling voice told all about the race against time of the *Seagull,* of the saving of the fleet, and hinted of deeper things best known only to the Zogo-le.

And the Zogo-le of Mer, Eroob, and Ugar declared through the Mamooses, that Bogo, son of Marboo, Chief of Las, and Wak, son of Duppa of the Sea Eagle clan, were now full warriors of Mer; and for all time were entitled to wear the sea eagle feather, and the dibi dibi pendant of warriorhood.

A mighty cheer arose, and the chiefs, then the warriors, then all the people pressed forward in congratulation. Bogo was in the seventh heaven of delight, and Jack was happy.

The boys remained honoured guests at Eroob for several months until the trading fleet was sighted. That was a time of rejoicing and excitement;

for the trade had been very successful, the fleet returning with new canoes loaded with weapons, hardwoods, sago, rattans, bundles of magnificent feathers and many other eagerly sought-after articles which the jungles of New Guinea supply.

The men of Mer were anxious to return home. Several days later the *Seagull* sailed with them, and next afternoon saw the bulk of Mer looming from the sea. Bogo nearly cried with delight.

After a week of feasting an imposing ceremony was held, during which the Mamoose presented Bogo and Jack with the eagle-hawk feather, and hung around each lad's neck the coveted dibi dibi pendant. Thus each was now officially a warrior of Mer.

Mer resumed its usual life: tending to the gardens, to the Sai, to turtle-hunting and hunting for the sea-cow, to the cruises of the fishing-fleets.

One morning, Jack was working in Duppa's garden when a blast from the Boo startled him. He listened; the Boo blared out again and a man ran past him shouting "A Lamar ship!"

Jack stared unbelievingly, then turned and raced down the path towards the beach. Upon an open hillside he stood and held his breath.

A sail! A ship coming straight for Mer.

His heart beat rapidly. A graceful three-masted brig in full sail! As she drew in towards dangerous waters, cautiously she shortened sail. Jack raced down to the beach. A great crowd was gathering excitedly, arguing. Would the Zogo-le attack the Lamars? How many of the fighting-men were here? How many away on the other side of the island? How many away with the fishing canoes? And what were the Lamars going to do?

The Lamars knew their business. Kept a safe distance from the shore, kept clear of dangerous reefs and current. Then down came the sails with the crews manning the yards like monkeys; the anchor splashed overboard; the chain rattled out. She was too far away for canoes to surprise her either by night or day. She was taking no chances.

The islanders were very disappointed. They knew the "fire-sticks" of the Lamars, those terrible thunder weapons that could kill at great distances. It was impossible to take a Lamar ship unless she struck a reef, or could be taken by surprise.

Then someone shouted, "Toree! Toree!" That was it. Iron, iron. The Lamars had come to trade perhaps. If so, here was a chance to trade for that priceless article—iron.

They ran back to the palms and hid their larger weapons, hastily loaded the smaller canoes with coconuts and tortoise-shell and anything they could lay hands on, and paddled out towards the ship.

A man stood in each bow waving a palm branch as he shouted "Poud!

Poud!" (Peace! Peace!) Then they all shouted "Toree! Toree!" (Iron! Iron!)

When near the ship sailors waved them to stand by. They ceased paddling. Then a canoe was signalled to approach close. She did so, her crew holding up tortoise-shell and shouting "Toree! Toree!"

Sailors held up pieces of iron.

The canoe drew near, sailors with their eyes searched the canoe for weapons, then satisfied, commenced to trade. They then waved the canoe away and beckoned another to come alongside, but all the other canoes were waved aside.

Jack saw the name "Mangles" upon the graceful bow, saw all the familiar life aboard ship, everything came back in a rush of memory. How different this life to the life of bow and arrow, of fish-spear and bone dagger. He stared at the ship, at the white faces and bared chests and arms; listened to British voices as a hungry man waits for food. He felt tongue-tied, he wanted to shout and tell them all about himself and young Will D'Oyly and about the *Charles Eaton.* He could not ^understand what was the matter, for each time he opened his mouth the words would not come. Suddenly, he realized he had almost forgotten his own language. In misery he waited, trying to form words as, slowly, canoe after canoe went forward to trade.

At last, he noticed the men aboard ship staring across to his canoe. The captain had noticed his brown skin was whiter than the others. Then came a shout. "Ahoy there redskin! What name you?"

"Wak!" shouted Ireland.

"Wak who?"

"Jack... Jack Ireland! He could hardly believe his ears as a torrent of native words left his lips mixed with the words "wreck", "Will D'Oyly", "Charles Eaton!"

Officers and crew were listening now: "Jack Ireland," "Will D'Oyly," "wreck," and "Charles Eaton" were English.

"Charles Eaton!" said Captain Carr wonderingly, "why that must be the *Charles Eaton* wrecked in Torres Strait several years ago, wasn't it? Do you remember a write-up in the *Madras Times* about it? Why, yes, of course! Didn't the Dutch rescue a few men who escaped in the boat?"

"Yes," answered the mate eagerly. "Ask him if he's a survivor from the *Charles Eaton."*

Captain Carr shouted the question and Jack shouted "Yes," in Mer language. "Yes, yes!" he shouted in English.

"Are there any more of you on the island?"

"Yes. Will D'Oyly."

"Where is he?"

"Away on the other side of the island with Oby."

"Who is Oby?"

"His father."

"His father?"

"Yes."

"Then Captain D'Oyly is alive."

"No, no," said Jack lapsing into excited island language again only to realize he was trying to tell them in native all about Oby, and the islanders' customs of adoption.

Captain Carr and the mate and crew were naturally puzzled. The more questions they asked, the more puzzled were they by the replies. At last the captain shouted: "How many survivors are there from the wreck."

"Four."

"Who are they?"

"Will D'Oyly, George D'Oyly, John Sexton, and me."

"Where are John Sexton and George D'Oyly?"

"I don't know." And Jack went back into native language again, trying to explain. Then motioned the canoemen to pull forward. As the canoe spurted to the ship's side he shouted, "Throw me a rope!"

But the other canoes all surged forward, for the men thought everything was all right now that Wak was going to board the ship. The crew became instantly alarmed; a sailor snatched up a cutlass and flourished it, men sprang to arms, guns poked out over the sides.

The canoes turned and fled. Sullenly they pulled back to the beach.

That evening they discussed the situation, certain the Lamars meant treachery. Waving palm branches of peace, they had paddled forward to trade when suddenly the ship bristled with guns.

If the Lamars were so ready for war as that, then, when they had won all the trade goods, might they not suddenly turn their thunder-sticks on the canoes, kill all the men, take back their iron, then land on Mer and burn the villages. Angrily they decided that this was so.

Jack volunteered to take the *Seagull* with Bogo and row out to the ship and explain, but Duppa seized his arm and fiercely exclaimed, "You shall not row out there to be killed!"

And the people immediately shouted assent. Then the Mamoose stepped forward, and the chiefs gathered around him. They commenced planning how best to defend the island.

Next day, by means of heavily armed boats, warily pulling towards the island, Captain Carr of the *Mangles* again tried to get in contact with the men of Mer. His object was to trade, and to learn more of the castaways, to trade for them if possible.

But the boats would not pull to the beach and the canoes would not sail out to them. The people kept behind their stockade, and the crews in the boats shouted from the water. In such distrust nothing could be gained, while violence was certain to be brewing.

Captain Carr finally ordered the boats back to the ship. Jack listened to the old sea-chanty as the crew manned the windlass. Up came the anchor, up rattled the sails, and the *Mangles* bore away.

Jack was bitterly disappointed. Another ship might not call again for years and years, perhaps not until he was an old man.

In a few weeks he got over his disappointment, for he had so many other things to think about, so much work to do.

But that visit of the *Mangles* meant that rescue was slowly but surely coming. The *Mangles* cruised away on its trading trip through the Strait, then on to the Dutch East Indies. In course of time the ship returned to Hong Kong and Canton. The captain reported the story of a white boy among the savages of Mer. The boy said he was Jack Ireland a survivor of the *Charles Eaton.* That young Will D'Oyly, son of a passenger, was with him. And that two other boys, George D'Oyly and John Sexton, were believed to be held prisoners somewhere with savages among the islands.

The news was forwarded to London and Sydney, and arrived in due course. The government of New South Wales then fitted out a schooner, the *Isabella,* under command of Captain C. M. Lewis. She was to sail to the Coral Sea, thence to the island of Mer and rescue, if possible, any survivors of the *Charles Eaton,* who might be held prisoners by the savages.

At the same time, the East India Company also sent their armed sloop, *Tigris,* under Captain Iggleston, to join in the search. Thus the *Tigris* sailed from Bombay in India, when the *Isabella* sailed from Sydney.

But Jack knew nothing about all this. It was a long time indeed after the *Mangles* left Mer before the rescue ships, sailing from different directions, were to enter the treacherous waters of the Coral Sea.

Meanwhile Jack tended his garden, and hunted the seas with Bogo. But over Jack and young Will D'Oyly there yet hovered the vengeance of Cut-cut.

The Schooner Isabella in Search of the Survivors.

The hut wherein lies the skull trophy.

23

RESCUE

The adventures of Jack Ireland and young Will D'Oyly are now drawing to a close. But, as I told you earlier in this book, everything written here is true. And the story would not be complete without the lads' last big adventure.

One morning Jack and several lads with young Ewas and half a dozen small boys paddled across to Dauar Isle. This tiny, hillocky island lies only a few hundred yards from the shores of Mer. Separating the rugged little isle from Waiar Isle is a reef broken by a channel. During the low tides it is almost possible to wade from isle to isle, only the channel has to be swum, or canoed across. At this season of the year a special shellfish appears around the shores of Dauar and Waiar. The people eagerly sought this shellfish. But inland from its shores the ill-omened isle of Waiar was taboo, the home of the dread god Waiat and his initiates. This god Waiat was not a carved figure, but was a giant of a man, the Chief of the Cult, and an enemy of Cut-cut. Though the people eagerly prowled the shores of Waiar, none dared enter among the pinnacles and chasms and gloomy arches and washed-out caverns which give such a weird appearance to the isle.

The boys had hardly landed on Dauar when a frightened lad came running.

"Wak! Ewas! Quick! the skull-hunters! Come for you! Quick!"

As they dashed for the canoe a wild yell rang out behind. They leaped in and paddled off as the oldest lad cried:

"Wak it is you and Ewas they seek! They will cut us off before we reach Mer. Best hide on Waiar, Wak, while we race to Mer for help."

"Right! across the channel," cried Jack. And the canoe swerved and cut straight for Waiar, hardly a bowshot away. Jack got a glimpse of the war canoe of the chief of Aureed, saw the gigantic form of Cut-cut urging the paddlers. As Jack and Ewas leaped out and splashed toward Waiar the lads' canoe pushed off and raced for Mer. Jack lifted Ewas and ran for his life. If he could only hide deep within Waiar he was safe. Help would be swift for already he heard an alarm booing from the height of Gelam-Pit. He splashed in among rocks frowning like giant sentinels then diving under an arch raced through a sea-worn cavern out into a mighty funnel with the sky shining above. Broken ramparts frowned down upon him where stone columns like fallen soldiers lay in the shallow water.

He raced for a cavern that twisted into a roofed chamber where sunlight gleamed through cracks, like loopholes in a castle. He hurried up what looked like a rough path that narrowed to a ledge winding beside a chasm falling sheer to some gurgle of the sea. Along the opposite wall rocks stood on end like pillars that once supported a mighty roof. Wherever daylight streamed in it fell upon mummified men trussed to bamboo poles. They glared down at him from gleaming eyes of pearl. He hesitated, but the clinging body of little Ewas urged him deeper into the very stronghold of the dread god Waiat.

Ewas did not whimper; he knew only too well what was coming. Jack, panting, stared wildly around. There arose a gurgling, a distressed moaning that was the tide in subterranean chambers sighing through vent-holes which led up to these fantastic rocks. He sped through gathering gloom under another arch, and a spiral ledge was before him. He began to climb, going higher and higher in a giant spiral that clung to a funnel that really was the remains of a blown-out volcano. He saw that there spiralled above his head a similar ledge like a narrow roof, and wondered if it were possible to walk up there too. He paused and, glancing below, saw the giant figure of Cut-cut with Biskea and four Aureed men at his heels. They were tracking him by his wet feet! And his only weapon was a fish-spear.

Despairingly he climbed up, seeking some cranny in the ledge where he might hide Ewas. If only he could save Ewas!

Then his heart sank. Ledge and wall ended sheer; a chasm separated him from a towering wall ahead.

He put Ewas down beside him.

"Keep your back to the wall Ewas," he panted. "Don't look down. Never fear. Oby and Duppa and Bogo will save us soon." He stared wildly around, then up. The ledge overhead ended abruptly too. Filled with a sudden wild hope he stared. Could he but spring up and grasp the end of that ledge then Ewas could climb up his legs, up over his body and shoulders, and crawl back on to the ledge. His heart thumped with hope. If only he could do it, then follow Ewas! They could creep back down that ledge which must lead right above this one straight back the way they had come.

Bracing himself he leaped up, his fingers easily gripped the edge of the ledge. He pulled himself up chest high and glanced along it—straight at the god Waiat.

From behind the terrible mask gleamed two malevolent eyes. The huge figure clad in-the terrifying dress of Waiat towered in the gloom against the wall. Great hands grasped a heavy black spear; its barbed spear-head gleamed dully and as dully Jack wondered why. Then stared in icy fear.

Between Waiat's feet was a circular hole in the ledge up which dim light shone upon the spear. Jack's head had passed directly below that hole, only two feet below that terrible spear. The god Waiat must have glared down at him as he passed underneath.

Why had he not struck?

A sudden wild hope set Jack's heart pounding, he remembered Bogo telling him that Waiat hated Cut-cut. Then he felt a frantic clutch at his legs. He lowered himself back to the ledge beside Ewas.

Cut-cut with Biskea close behind were almost upon them. Cut-cut shook his club with a horrible grimace; he would have loved to yell a war-cry and charge, but the taboo upon this evil stronghold weighed too heavily upon him. He crouched forward to end it. quickly. Jack swung back his fish-spear, held his breath. He could see the little black rim of the hole now almost above Cut-cut's head. Cut-cut crouched forward and laughed silently. It was the last time Jack was to stare into those terrible eyes with their violent circles of yellow, see that mouth twitching in hideous mirth. Cut-cut saw the chasm behind Jack, saw he dared neither spring back nor aside. He slung his club and thrust his long spear before him. He would simply advance and his victim must take the spear or leap—or both!

He crouched forward and his grin jarred on clenched teeth, his eyes jumped big as a spear came straight down on his head. He slid sideways and over to a sound like rushing air. Then a dull thud far below.

Not a sound, except the muffled thump of Jack's heart and a moan of water through some subterranean air-pipe.

Biskea stood open-mouthed, bewildered. He shuddered, turned and whispered. Then Jack saw his retreating back.

Jack waited awhile. There was a deathly silence over all, the feeling as of some threatening presence. He lifted the trembling Ewas.

"Don't murmur Ewas," he whispered, "we must chance it. I believe we're safe."

He started walking steadily down the ledge, felt his heart thumping as he neared that hole above. He passed under it with no quickening of his steps, stepped on and then could almost have cried with relief. Nothing had happened.

When he got out of that evil place and into God's own sunlight again the skull-hunters were leaping into their canoe—with the *Sea Eagle* coming swiftly.

There is but little more to tell of Jack Ireland and young Will D'Oyly. That last attempt against them by the Aureed skull-hunters was their last big adventure. Soon afterwards the sails of the *Isabella* appeared. She anchored close by Mer.

The men of Mer watched her sullenly. Captain Lewis had been given strict orders by the New South Wales authorities to treat the islanders with every consideration. To try and ransom any prisoners, and promise the islanders that for any future castaways they rescued, a big ransom would be paid. However, if there were any castaways among the savages and they would not give them up, then the castaways were to be taken by force.

Captain Lewis sent armed boats ashore with peaceful messages and gifts of iron. At last the men of Mer detailed Jack to speak for them.

Captain Lewis's task was easy then. He asked Jack to tell the Mamoose he was come for the two white boys. He would pay a heavy ransom; he showed them cases of tomahawks, such iron as the islanders had never seen. But he must have the boys.

Then followed some days of haggling. Duppa and Oby did not want to give up the boys. Young Ewas clung to Oby and sobbed, refusing ever to leave him. Old Duppa placed his hands on Jack's shoulders.

"You surely do not wish to leave me, Wak?" he asked, "to leave me and Pamoy and Mer, and go back to the Lamars?"

Bogo looked on silently, and Jack was bewildered. He wondered about young Will D'Oyly: the boy was perfectly happy. His own mother and father were dead. He knew no other life now than that of these people. And he loved them.

Captain Lewis at last persuaded Duppa and Oby to go aboard the *Isabella.* Patiently he explained to them, through Jack, that he must have the boys.

The next day, quietly he showed the islanders what his big guns could do. The Zogo-le settled it. They ordered that, for the sake of the peace of the island, the boys be returned to the Lamar ship. But that the ransom be doubled.

The leave-taking was very unhappy. Young Ewas clung to Oby, until at last Oby thrust him aside and leaped overboard. Duppa placed his hands on Jack's shoulders, looked unhappily into his eyes, then abruptly turned his back and followed Oby.

When the *Isabella* sailed, Jack gazed unhappily at Mer, slowly fading away. He gazed until Gelam even faded from sight. He knew now that he loved Mer. With unhappy heart he said farewell.

Captain Lewis, by kind questioning, had got almost all the story. He

Duppa taking leave of the boys on the *Isabella*.

Captain Lewis buried the skulls under this tree.

was sailing now for Eroob, to search for other survivors. Although Jack had assured him that there were none there.

Unhappily Jack realized that these men could only partly understand him; he had heard the crew whisper that he was "native", that he was nearly a half-wit after his life among the savages. He spoke haltingly in English with many words of Mer; he had already given up trying to explain to these men numerous customs of the islanders which he understood so well. He now realized they would never understand. They called him a half-wit—he who was a warrior of Mer and he wondered what sort of a life lay ahead of him, when once he reached civilization again.

A heavy wind sprang up, unusual for that period of the year. It drove the *Isabella* on to Canoe Cay, a great sandbank, where she was nearly lost. For a week then she had to stand to, fearful of venturing until the weather quietened.

The captain asked Jack if this weather was not unusual.

"Yes. The Zogo-le have made the big wind, because they are angry at you having taken us from Mer." And he would not explain further.

"Let them call me a half-wit," he muttered. "They would never understand."

No survivors were found on Eroob. When the captain asked them where were John Sexton and George D'Oyly, they could only tell him what they had heard: that the boys had been killed.

Jack noticed a number of Aureed men crouching away among the Erubians. He knew these must be visitors and was not surprised when the canoe fled by night. The Aureed men would warn all the islanders about the coming of the Lamar ship.

Captain Lewis left a letter with the Mamoose and old Ag-ghe to give to Captain Iggleston of the sloop, *Tigris,* should she arrive. He rewarded them well with iron and impressed upon them that white ships would always give much iron for any castaways they saved. The *Isabella,* then sailed S.W. by S. for Aureed Island where, so Jack told Captain Lewis, he might get news of Sexton and D'Oyly.

But they never heard any more of the two boys. The Aureed men hastening from Eroob had spread news of the coming of a Lamar ship of war.

Every island they visited was deserted. When they came to Aureed they found the skulls around the Augud, in the Zogo-house. They took these last sad relics aboard the *Isabella,* burnt the Zogo-house; chopped down the palms; put a fire-stick to the island. Then sailed for Torres Strait.

At Double Island, the Isabella met the Tigris. She had called at Eroobon the heels of the *Isabella,* and the Mamoose and Ag-ghe had faithfully delivered Captain Lewis's message.

The course of the *Tigris* is now shown on our charts as Tigris Passage. The vessels sailed in company to Timor, where they parted. The *Tigris* sailing for India, the *Isabella* to Sydney.

At Sydney the skulls of the people of the *Charles Eaton* were buried at Bunnerong Cemetery, where they lie today.

And so ends the tragic but true story of Jack Ireland and Will D'Oyly, and their life and adventures among the savages.

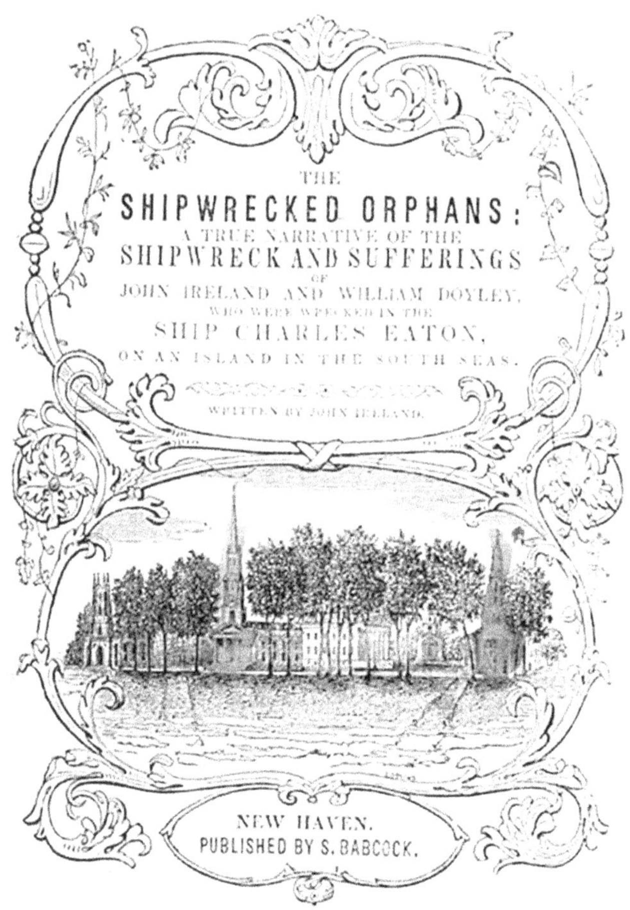

LIST OF PASSENGERS AND CREW OF THE *CHARLES EATON*

GEORGE FREDRIC MOORE, **Master.**
F. CLARE, **Chief Mate.**
W. MAYER, **Second mate.**
—. PYALL, **Third mate.**
G. PIGOTT, **Bosun.**
J. GRANT, **Surgeon.**
L. CONSTANTINE, **Carpenter.**
W. MONTGOMERY, **Steward.**
W. PERRY, **Midshipman.**
TOMMY CHENG, **Midshipman.**
S. BAYLETT, **Seaman.**
R. QUIN, **Seaman.**
A. QUAIL, **Seaman.**
W. MOORE, **Seaman.**
J. CAEN, **Seaman.**
WILL HILL, **Seaman.**
J. BERRY, **Seaman.**
G. LOURNE, **Seaman.**
W. JEFFREY, **Seaman.**
J. WRIGHT, **Seaman.**
W. GUMBLE, **Seaman.**
J. MILLER, **Seaman.**
W. WILLIAMS, **Seaman.**
C. ROBINSON, **Seaman.**
J. PRICE, **Seaman.**
J. SEXTON, **Steward's boy.**
J. IRELAND, **Cabin boy.**
C. G. ARMSTRONG, **Passenger.**
CAPTAIN D'OYLY, **Passenger.**
MRS D'OYLY, **Passenger.**
GEORGE D'OYLY, **Passenger.**
W. T. O. D'OYLY, **Passenger.**
ONE NATIVE INDIAN MEM-SERVANT.

Escaped in Boat to Timor Laut and Eventually Rescued by the Dutch
G. Pigott, died of hardships.
J. Wright.
Laurie Constantine.
W. Gumble.
R. Quin.

Rescued by the "Isabella"
John Ireland.
William T. D'Oyly.

THE TOMB AT BUNNERONG CEMETERY, SYDNEY. THE ONLY EXISTING MEMORIAL OF THE TRAGEDY THAT IS THE THEME OF THIS BOOK

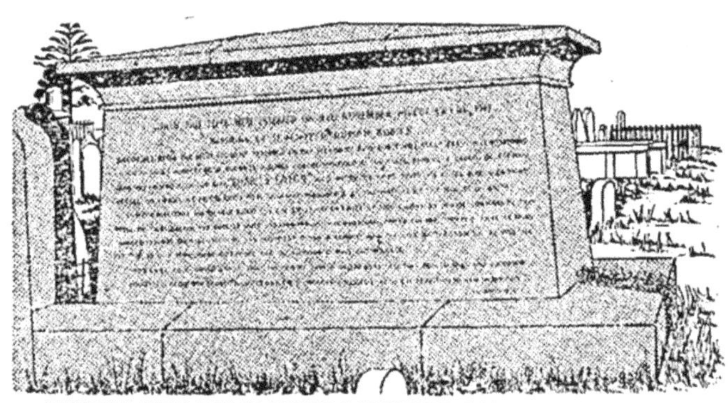

WITHIN THIS TOMB WERE INTERRED ON XVII NOVEMBER, MDCCCXXXVI, THE REMAINS OF SEVENTEEN HUMAN BODIES

Discovered after the most diligent research in the island of Aureed in Torres Strait, by Mr C. M. Lewis, Commander of H.M. Colonial Schooner *Isabella,* and by satisfactory evidence identified as the mortal remains of certain of the officers, crew and passengers of the bark *Charles Eaton,* who, after escaping from the total wreck of that vessel on XV August, MDCCCXXXIV, were savagely massacred by the natives of the islands on which they landed.

His Excellency Sir Richard Bourke, K.C.B., Governor in Chief of this colony, by whose command the expedition to ascertain the fate of these unhappy persons was undertaken, caused the last offices of piety to be discharged toward them, by directing the internment of their remains with the rites of Christian burial, and the erection of this monument to record the catastrophe by which they perished.

"And they told David, saying, that the men of Jabesh-Gilead were they that buried Saul. And David sent messengers to the men of Jabesh-Gilead, and said unto them, Blessed be ye of the Lord, that ye have shown this kindness." —II Sam. ii, 4-2

ION IDRIESS BOOKS Available from
ETT Imprint

PROSPECTING FOR GOLD
LASSETER'S LAST RIDE
FLYNN OF THE INLAND
THE DESERT COLUMN
HORRIE THE WOG DOG
DRUMS OF MER
THE RED CHIEF
NEMARLUK
MADMAN'S ISLAND
THE YELLOW JOSS
THE SILVER CITY
FORTY FATHOMS DEEP
GOLD-DUST AND ASHES
LIGHTNING RIDGE
THE WILD WHITE MAN OF BADU
HEADHUNTERS OF THE CORAL SEA
SHOOT TO KILL
SNIPING
GUERRILLA TACTICS
ION IDRIESS: The Last Interview

forthcoming

THE SCOUT
LURKING DEATH
TRAPPING THE JAP

www.ingramcontent.com/pod-product-compliance
Ingram Content Group Australia Pty Ltd
76 Discovery Rd, Dandenong South VIC 3175, AU
AUHW020837290126
422694AU00002B/39

9 781923 024755